Penguin Books

The Easy Way to
Stop Smoking

Allen Carr

THE EASY WAY TO STOP SMOKING

PENGUIN BOOKS

Penguin Books Ltd, Harmondsworth, Middlesex, England
Viking Penguin Inc., 40 West 23rd Street, New York, New York 10010, U.S.A.
Penguin Books Australia Ltd, Ringwood, Victoria, Australia
Penguin Books Canada Ltd, 2801 John Street, Markham, Ontario, Canada L3R 1B4
Penguin Books (N.Z.) Ltd, 182–190 Wairau Road, Auckland 10, New Zealand

First published privately by Allen Carr 1985
Published in Penguin Books 1987

Designed by Aardvark, Thames Wharf Studios, Rainville Road, London W6 9HA

Filmset in Linotype Century Schoolbook

Reproduced, printed and bound in Great Britain by
Hazell Watson & Viney Limited,
Member of the BPCC Group,
Aylesbury, Bucks

Dedication

I dedicate this book to the 16 to 20 per cent that I have failed to cure. I hope it will help them to "kick the habit".

And to Sid.

Contents

Introduction

At last the miracle cure all smokers have been waiting for:

- ★ Instantaneous.
- ★ Equally effective for the heavy smoker.
- ★ No bad withdrawal pangs.
- ★ Needs no willpower.
- ★ No shock treatment.
- ★ No aids or gimmicks required.
- ★ You will not even put on weight.
- ★ Permanent.

If you are a smoker all you have to do is read on.

If you are a non-smoker purchasing for a loved one all you have to do is to persuade them to read the book. If you cannot persuade them, then read the book yourself and the last chapter will advise you how to get the message across, also how to prevent your children from starting. Do not be fooled by the fact that they hate it now, all children do before they become hooked.

1

The Worst Nicotine Addict
I Have Yet to Meet

Perhaps I should begin with detailing my competency for writing this book. No I am not a doctor or a psychiatrist, my qualifications are far more effective. I spent 25 years of my life as a confirmed smoker. In the later years I smoked a hundred a day on a bad day, and never less than 60.

During my life I had made dozens of attempts to stop. I once stopped for six months and I was still climbing-up the wall; still standing near smokers trying to get a whiff of the tobacco; still travelling in the smokers compartments on trains.

With most smokers, on the health side, it's a question of "I'll stop before it happens to me". I had reached the stage where I knew it was killing me. I had a permanent headache with the pressure of the constant coughing. I could feel the continuous throbbing in the vein that runs vertically down the centre of the forehead and I honestly believed that any moment there would be an explosion in my head and that I would die from a brain haemorrhage. It bothered me but it still didn't stop me.

I had reached the stage where I gave up even trying to stop. It was not so much that I enjoyed smoking. Most smokers have suffered the illusion sometime in their lives that they enjoy the odd cigarette, but I never suffered that illusion. I have always detested the taste and smell but I thought a cigarette helped me to relax. It gave me courage and confidence and I was always so miserable when I tried to stop, never being able to visualise an enjoyable life without a cigarette.

Eventually my wife sent me to a hypnotherapist. I must confess that I was completely sceptical, knowing nothing about hypnosis in those days and having visions of a Svengali-type figure with piercing eyes and waving pendula. I had all the normal illusions that smokers have about smoking except one – I knew that I wasn't a weak-willed person. With all other events in my life I was in control. With cigarettes they controlled me. I thought that hypnosis involved the forcing of wills and

1

although not obstructive (like most smokers I dearly wanted to stop), I thought no one was going to kid me that I didn't need to smoke.

The whole session appeared to be a waste of time. The hypnotherapist tried to make me lift my arms, and do various other things. Nothing appeared to be working properly, I didn't lose consciousness, I didn't go into a trance or at least I didn't think I did and yet after that session, not only did I stop smoking, I actually enjoyed the process even during the withdrawal period.

During those awful years as a smoker I thought that my life depended on those cigarettes and I was prepared to die rather than be without them. Today people ask me whether I ever have the odd pang. The answer is, "never, never, never", just the reverse. I've had a marvellous life. If I had died through smoking I couldn't have complained. I have been a very lucky man, but the most marvellous thing that has ever happened to me is being freed from that nightmare, that slavery of having to go through life systematically destroying your own body and having to pay through the nose for the privilege.

Let me make it quite clear from the beginning, I am not a mystical figure. I do not believe in magicians or fairies. I have a scientific brain and I couldn't understand what appeared to me like magic. I started reading up on hypnosis and on smoking. Nothing I read seemed to explain the miracle that had happened, i.e. why it had been so ridiculously easy to stop whereas previously it had been weeks of black depression?

It took me a long time to work it all out, basically because I was going about it back to front. I was trying to work out why it had been so easy to stop, whereas the real problem is trying to *explain* why smokers find it difficult to stop. Smokers talk about the terrible withdrawal pangs but when I looked back and tried to remember those awful pangs, they didn't exist for me. There was no physical pain, it was all in the mind.

My full time profession is now helping other people to kick the habit. My success rate is in excess of 80 per cent. I have helped to cure thousands of smokers and, let me emphasise from the start, there is no such thing as a confirmed smoker. I have still not met anybody that was as badly hooked, or rather, thought he was as badly hooked as myself. Anybody can not only stop smoking, but find it easy to stop. It is basically fear that keeps us smoking. The fear that life will never be quite as enjoyable without cigarettes and the fear of feeling deprived. In fact, nothing could be further from the truth. Not only is life just as enjoyable without them, it is infinitely more so in so many ways and the extra health, energy, and wealth are the least of the advantages.

All smokers can find it easy to stop smoking, even you! All you have to do is read the rest of the book with an open mind. The more you can understand, the easier you will find it. Even if you do not understand a word, provided you follow the instructions, you will find it easy. Most important of all, you will not go through life moping about cigarettes or feeling deprived. In fact, the only mystery will be why you did it for so long.

Let me issue a warning. There are only two reasons for failure under my method:

1 **FAILURE TO CARRY OUT INSTRUCTIONS:** Some people find it annoying that I am so dogmatic about certain recommendations. For example, I will tell you not to try cutting-down or to use substitutes like sweets, chewing gum etc. (particularly anything containing nicotine). The reason that I am so dogmatic is because I know my subject. I do not deny that there are many people that have succeeded in stopping using such ruses, but they have succeeded in spite of, not because of, them. There are people that can make love standing on a hammock but it is not the easiest way. Everything I tell you has a purpose to make it easy to stop and thereby ensure success.

2 **FAILURE TO UNDERSTAND:** Do not take anything for granted. Question not only what I tell you but question your own views and what society has taught you about smoking. For example those of you that think it is just a habit, do not just assume it. Ask yourselves why other habits, some of them enjoyable ones, are easy to break? Yet a habit that tastes awful, costs us a fortune, and kills us, is so difficult to break?

Those of you that think you enjoy a cigarette, ask yourselves why other things in life, which are infinitely more enjoyable, you can take or leave. Why is it with the cigarette you *have* to have it and panic sets in if you don't?

2

The Easy Method

The object of this book is to get you into the frame of mind that, instead of the normal method of stopping whereby you start off with the feeling that you are climbing Mount Everest and spend the next few weeks craving a cigarette and envying other smokers, you start right away with a feeling of elation like being cured from a terrible disease. From then on, the further you go through life, the more you will look at cigarettes and wonder how you ever smoked them in the first place. You will then look at smokers with pity as opposed to envy.

Provided that you are not a non-smoker or an ex-smoker, it is essential to keep smoking until you have finished the book completely. This may appear to be a contradiction. Later I shall be explaining that cigarettes do absolutely nothing for you at all. In fact one of the many conundrums about smoking is that when we are actually smoking the cigarette, we look at it and wonder why we are doing it. It is only when we have been deprived that the cigarette becomes precious. However, let us accept that whether you like it or not, you believe you are hooked. When you believe you are hooked, you can never be completely relaxed or concentrate properly unless you are smoking. So at this stage do not attempt to stop smoking before you have finished the whole book. As you read further into the book your desire to smoke will gradually be reduced. Do not go off half-cocked; this could be fatal. Remember all you have to do is to follow the instructions.

Basically my method is the complete opposite to the normal method of trying to stop. The *normal* method is to list the considerable disadvantages of smoking and say "If only I can go long enough without a cigarette, eventually the desire to smoke will go. I can then enjoy life again free of the slavery of the weed."

This is the logical way to go about it and thousands of smokers are stopping every day using variations of this method. However it is very difficult to succeed using this method for the following reasons:

1 Stopping smoking is not the real problem. Every time you put a cigarette out you stop smoking. You may have powerful reasons

4

on day one to say "I do not want to smoke any more" – all smokers have the whole of their lives and the reasons are more powerful than you can possibly imagine. The real problem is day two, day ten, or day ten thousand when, in a weak moment, an inebriated moment, or even a strong moment, you have one cigarette and, because it is partly drug addiction, you then want another and suddenly you are a smoker again.

2 The health scares should stop us, our rational minds say: "stop doing it, you are a fool", but in fact they make it harder. We smoke, for example, when we are nervous. Tell smokers that it is killing them and the first thing they will do is to light a cigarette. There are more dog ends outside the Royal Marsden Hospital, the country's foremost cancer treatment establishment, than any other hospital in the country.

3 All reasons for stopping actually make it harder for two others reasons:
Firstly they create this feeling of sacrifice. We are always being forced to give up our little friend, or prop or vice or pleasure whichever way the smoker sees it.
Secondly it creates a "Blind". We do not smoke for the reasons we should stop, the real problem is "Why do we want or need to do it?"

The Easy Method is basically this. Initially to forget the reasons we'd like to stop; to face the cigarette problem and ask ourselves the following questions:

1 What is it doing for me?
2 Do I actually enjoy it?
3 Do I really need to go through life paying through the nose just to stick these things in my mouth and suffocate myself?

The beautiful truth is that it does absolutely nothing for you at all. Let me make it quite clear I do not mean the disadvantages of being a smoker outweigh the advantages, all smokers know that all their lives. I mean there are not *any* advantages from smoking. The only advantage it ever had was the social "plus"; nowadays even smokers themselves regard it as an anti-social habit.

Most smokers find it necessary to rationalise why they smoke but the reasons are all fallacies and illusions.

The first thing we are going to do is to remove these fallacies and illusions. In fact, you will realise that there is nothing to give up. Not only is there nothing to give up but that there are marvellous positive gains from being a non-smoker and that health and money are only part of these gains. Once the illusion that life will never be quite as enjoyable without the cigarette is removed, once you realise that not only is life just as enjoyable without it but infinitely more so, once the feeling of being deprived or of missing-out are eradicated, then we can go back to the health and money – and the dozens of other reasons for stopping smoking. These realisations will become positive additional aids to help you to achieve what you really desire – to enjoy the whole of your life free from the slavery of the weed.

3

Why is it Difficult to Stop?

As I explained earlier, I got interested in this subject because of my own addiction. When I finally stopped it was like magic. When I had previously tried to stop it was weeks of black depression. There would be odd days when I was comparatively cheerful and the next day back with the depression. It was like clawing your way out of a slippery pit, you feel you are near the top, you see the sunshine and then find yourself sliding down again. Eventually you light that cigarette, it tastes awful and you try to work out why you have to do it.

One of the questions I always ask smokers prior to my consultations is "Do you want to stop smoking?" In a way it is a stupid question. All smokers (including members of FOREST) would love to stop smoking. If you say to the most confirmed smoker "If you could go back to the time before you became hooked, with the knowledge you have now, would you have started smoking?" "NO WAY" is the reply.

Say to the most confirmed smoker i.e. someone that doesn't think that it injures his health, that is not worried about the social stigma and that can afford it (there are not many about these days) "Do you encourage your children to smoke?" "NO WAY" is the reply.

All smokers feel that something evil has got possession of them. In the early days it is a question of "I am going to stop, not today but tomorrow". Eventually we get to the stage where we think either we haven't got the willpower or that there is something inherent in us or the cigarette that we must have in order to enjoy life.

As I said previously the difficulty is not explaining why it is easy to stop *it is explaining why it is difficult*. In fact the real problem is explaining why anybody does it in the first place or how, at one time, over 60% of the population were smoking.

The whole business of smoking is an incredible enigma. The only reason we get onto it is because of the thousands of people already doing it. Yet every one of them wishes they had not started in the first place, telling us that it is a waste of time and money. We cannot quite believe they are not enjoying it. We associate it with being grown up and work so hard to become hooked ourselves. We then spend the rest of our lives telling our own children not to do it and trying to kick the habit ourselves.

We then spend the rest of our lives paying through the nose. The average 20-a-day smoker spends £25,000 in his/her lifetime on cigarettes. What do we do with that money (it wouldn't be so bad if we threw it down the drain)? We actually use it to systematically congest our lungs with cancerous tars, to progressively clutter-up and poison our blood vessels. Each day we are increasingly starving every muscle and organ of our bodies of oxygen, so that each day we become more lethargic. We sentence ourselves to a lifetime of filth, bad breathe, stained teeth, burnt clothes, filthy ashtrays and the foul smell of stale tobacco. It is a lifetime of slavery. We spend half our lives in situations in which society forbids us to smoke e.g. churches, hospitals, schools, tube trains, theatres etc. or in situations where we ourselves are trying to cut down or stop, feeling deprived. The rest of our smoking lives is spent in situations where we are allowed to smoke wishing we didn't have to. What sort of hobby is it that when you are doing it you wish you weren't and when you are not doing it you crave a cigarette? It's a lifetime of being treated by half of society like some sort of leper and, worst of all, a lifetime of an otherwise intelligent, rational human being going through life in contempt. The smoker despises himself, every budget day, every National Non-Smoking Day, everytime he inadvertently reads the government health warning or there is a cancer scare or a bad breath campaign, everytime he gets congested or has a pain in the chest, everytime he is the lone smoker in company with non-smokers. Having to go through life with these awful black shadows at the back of his mind, what does he get out of it? ABSOLUTELY NOTHING!!! The pleasure?, the enjoyment?, the relaxation?, the prop?, the boost?, all illusions, unless you consider the wearing of tight shoes to enjoy the removal of them as some sort of pleasure!

As I have said the real problem is trying to explain not only why smokers find it difficult to stop, but why anybody does it at all.

You are probably saying "That's all very well, I know this, but once you are hooked on these things it is very difficult to stop. But why is it so difficult, and why do we have to do it? Smokers search for the answer to these questions all of their lives.

Some say it is the powerful withdrawal symptoms from nicotine. In fact the actual withdrawn symptoms from nicotine are so mild (*see Chapter 6*), that most smokers have lived and died without ever realising they are drug addicts.

Some say cigarettes are very enjoyable. They aren't, they are filthy disgusting objects. Ask any smoker who thinks he only smokes because

8

he enjoys a cigarette if when he hasn't got his own brand and can only obtain a brand he finds distasteful, whether he stops smoking? In fact smokers would rather smoke old rope than not smoke at all. Enjoyment has nothing to do with it. I enjoy lobster but I never got to the stage where I had to have 20 Lobsters hanging round my neck. With other things in life we enjoy it whilst we are doing it but we don't sit feeling deprived when we are not.

Some search for deep psychological reasons, "the Freud syndrome", "The child at the mothers breast". Really it is just the reverse. The usual reason we start smoking is to show we are grown up and mature. If we had to suck a dummy in company we would die of embarrassment.

Some think it is the reverse, the *Macho* effect of breathing smoke or fire down your nostrils. Again this argument has no substance, a burning cigarette in the ear would appear ridiculous. How much more ridiculous to actually breathe cancer-triggering tars into your lungs.

Some say "it is something to do with my hands!" So, why light it?

"It is oral satisfaction." So, why light it?

"It is the feeling of the smoke going into my lungs." An awful feeling – it is called suffocation!

Many believe it relieves boredom. This is also a fallacy. Boredom is a frame of mind.

For 25 years my reason was that it relaxed me, gave me confidence and courage. I also knew it was killing me and costing me a fortune. Why didn't I go to my doctor and ask him for an alternative to relax me and give me courage and confidence? I didn't go because I knew he would suggest an alternative. It wasn't my reason, it was my excuse.

Some say they only do it because their friends do it. Are you really that stupid? If so, just pray that your friends do not start cutting their heads off to cure a headache!

Most smokers that think about it eventually come to the conclusion that it is just a habit. This is not really an explanation but having discounted all the usual rational explanations it appears to be the only remaining excuse. Unfortunately this explanation is equally illogical. Every day of our lives we change habits and some of them are very enjoyable. My eating habits relate back to my smoking days. I do not eat breakfast or lunch; just one meal a day in the evening. Yet when I go on holiday my favourite meal is breakfast. The day I return I revert back to my normal habit without the slightest effort.

What is it with a habit that tastes awful, that kills us, that costs us a fortune, that is filthy and disgusting and that we would dearly love to break anyway, when all we have to do is to stop doing it? Why is it so dif-

ficult? The answer is, it isn't. It is ridiculously easy. Once you understand the real reasons that you smoke you will stop doing it – just like
that – and, at the most, in three weeks' time the only mystery will be
why you smoked so long in the first place.

READ ON.

4

The Sinister Trap

Smoking is the most subtle, sinister trap in nature. Man could not begin to conceive of anything so ingenious. What gets us into it in the first place? The thousands of adults that are already doing it. They even warn us that it's a filthy disgusting habit that will eventually destroy us, and keep us poor for the rest of our lives, but we cannot believe that they are not enjoying it. One of the many pathetic aspects of the smoking habit is how hard we have to work in order to become hooked.

It is the only trap in nature which has no lure, no piece of cheese. The thing that springs the trap is not that cigarettes taste so marvellous, it's that they taste so awful. If that first cigarette tasted marvellous, alarm bells would ring and, as intelligent human beings, we could then understand why half the adult population was systematically paying through the nose to poison themselves. But because that first cigarette tastes awful our young minds are reassured that we will never become hooked and we think that, because we are not enjoying them, we can stop whenever we want to.

It is the only drug in nature where you never achieve what you set out to. Boys usually start because they want to appear tough – it is the Humphrey Bogart/Clint Eastwood image. The last think you feel with the first cigarette is tough. You dare not inhale and, if you have too many, you start to feel dizzy then sick. All you want to do is get away from the other boys and throw the filthy things away.

With women, it is to be the sophisticated modern young lady. We have all seen them taking little puffs on the cigarette looking absolutely ridiculous. By the time the boys have learnt to look tough and the girls have learnt to look sophisticated, they wish they had never started in the first place!

We then spend the rest of our lives trying to explain to ourselves why we do it, telling our children not to get caught, and, at odd times, trying to escape ourselves.

The trap is so designed that we only try to stop when we have stress in our lives, whether it be health, shortage of money or just plain being made to feel like a leper.

As soon as we stop we have more stress i.e. the fearful withdrawal pangs of nicotine and the thing that we rely on to relieve stress i.e. our old prop the cigarette, we now must do without.

After a few days of torture we decide that we have picked the wrong time, we must wait for a period without stress, and as soon as that arrives so the reason to stop goes. Of course that period will never arrive because in the first place our lives tend to become more and more stressful. As we leave the protection of our parents, the natural process is setting-up home, mortages, babies, more responsible jobs etc etc. At the same time smokers lives automatically become more stressful because tobacco does not relax you or relieve stress as society tries to make you believe, just the reverse, it actually causes you to become more nervous and distressed.

Even those smokers that kick the habit (most do, one or more times during their lives) can lead perfectly happy lives and suddenly become hooked again.

The whole business of smoking is like wandering into a giant maze. As soon as we enter the maze our minds become misted and clouded and we spend the rest of our lives trying to escape. Many of us eventually do, only to find that we get trapped again at a later date.

I spent 25 years trying to escape from that maze. Like all smokers I couldn't understand it either. However due to a combination of unusual circumstances, none of which reflect any credit on me, instead of most ex-smokers who are just grateful to have kicked the habit and just go on to enjoy their healthier and wealthier lives, I didn't. I wanted to know why it had been so desperately difficult to stop and yet when I finally did, it was not only easy but enjoyable.

Since stopping smoking my life's hobby and eventually my profession has been to answer the many conundrums about smoking. It is a complex and facinating puzzle and like the rubic cube – practically impossible to solve. However like all complicated puzzles, if you know the solution, it is easy! I have the solution to make stopping smoking easy. I will lead you out of the maze and ensure that you never wander into it again. All you have to do is *follow the instructions*. If you take a wrong turn the rest of the instructions will be pointless!

Let me emphasise that anybody can find it easy to stop smoking but first we need to remove some of the illusions about the facts. No I do not mean the scare facts, I know you are already aware of them. There are already enough books and information on the evils of smoking. If that was going to stop you, you would already have stopped. I mean why do we find it difficult to stop? In order to answer this we need to know the true reason why we are still smoking.

5

Why Do We Carry on Smoking?

We all start smoking for stupid reasons usually due to social pressures or social occasions; but, once we feel we are becoming hooked, why do we carry on smoking?

No regular smokers know why they smoke. If they knew the true reason, they would stop doing it. I have asked this question of thousands of smokers during my consultations. The true answer is the same for all smokers but the variety of replies are infinite. I find this part of the consultation at the same time the most amusing and the most pathetic.

All smokers know in their heart of hearts that they are mugs. They know that they had no need to smoke before they became hooked. Most of them can remember their first cigarette tasted awful and that they had to work hard in order to become hooked. The most annoying part is that they sense that non-smokers are not missing anything and that non-smokers are laughing at them (it is difficult not to on Budget days).

However smokers are intelligent, rational human beings. They know that they are taking enormous health risks and that they spend a fortune in their lifetime on cigarettes. Therefore it is necessary for them to have a rational explanation to justify these risks.

The actual reasons why smokers continue to smoke are a subtle combination of the factors which I will elaborate in the next two chapters. They are:

1 NICOTINE ADDICTION
2 BRAINWASHING

6

Nicotine Addiction

Nicotine is a colourless, oily compound and is the drug contained in tobacco which addicts the smoker. It is the fastest addictive drug known to mankind and it can take just one cigarette to become hooked.

Every puff on a cigarette delivers, via the lungs to the brain, a small dose of nicotine more rapidly than the dose of heroin the addict injects into his veins.

If there are twenty puffs for you in one cigarette you receive 20 doses of the drug with just one cigarette.

Nicotine is a quick acting drug and levels in the bloodstream fall quickly to about half within 30 minutes of smoking a cigarette and to only a quarter within an hour of finishing a cigarette. This explains why most smokers average about 20 per day.

As soon as the smoker extinguishes the cigarette, the nicotine rapidly starts to leave the body and the smoker begins to suffer withdrawal pangs.

I must at this point dispel a common illusion that smokers have about withdrawal pangs. Smokers think that withdrawal pangs are the terrible trauma they suffer when they try to stop smoking or are forced to stop smoking. This is in fact mainly mental and is due to the smoker feeling deprived of his pleasure or prop. I will explain more about this later.

The actual withdrawal pangs from nicotine are so subtle that most smokers have lived and died without even realising they are drug addicts. When we use the term "Nicotine Addicts" we think we just got into "the habit". Most smokers have a horror of drugs and yet that's exactly what they are – drug addicts. Fortunately it is an easy drug to kick but you need to first accept that you are addicted.

There is no physical pain in the withdrawal pangs from nicotine. It is merely an empty, restless feeling, the feeling of something missing, which is why many smokers think it is something to do with hands. If it is prolonged the smoker becomes nervous, insecure agitated, lacking in confidence and irritable. It is like a hunger not for food, but for a poison – NICOTINE

Within seven seconds of lighting a cigarette, fresh nicotine is supplied and the craving ends resulting in the feeling of relaxation and confidence that the cigarette gives to the smoker.

In the early days when we start smoking the withdrawal pangs and the relief of them are so slight that we are not even aware that they exist. For most people the very first cigarettes are smoked, if you are a boy, to be 'Jack The Lad'. If you are a girl, to be the sophisticated young lady.

When we begin to smoke regularly we think it is because either we've come to enjoy them or that it is just that we have got into "the habit". The truth is we're already hooked; we do not realise it but that little nicotine monster is already inside our stomach and every now and again we have to feed it.

All smokers start smoking for stupid reasons, nobody has to. The only reason anybody continues smoking whether they be a casual smoker or a heavy smoker is to feed that little monster.

The whole business of smoking is a series of conundrums. All smokers know at heart they are mugs and that they have been trapped by something evil. However, I think the most pathetic aspect of all about smoking is that the actual feeling of enjoyment that the smoker gets from a cigarette is the pleasure of trying to get back to the state of peace, tranquillity and confidence that his body had before he became hooked in the first place.

You know that feeling when a neighbour's burglar alarm has been ringing all day, or some other minor, persistent aggravation. You are not aware of it but then the noise suddenly stops – that marvellous feeling of peace and tranquillity is experienced. It is not really peace but the ending of the aggravation.

Before we start the nicotine chain our bodies are complete, we then put nicotine into the body and when we put that cigarette out and the nicotine starts to leave, we suffer withdrawal pangs – no physical pain just an empty feeling. We are not even aware that it exists but it is like a dripping tap inside our bodies. Our rational minds do not understand it. They do not need to. All we know is that we want a cigarette and when we light it, the craving goes and for the moment we are content and confident again just like we were before we became addicted. However the satisfaction is only temporary, because in order to relieve the craving, you have to put more nicotine into the body. As soon as you extinguish that cigarette, the craving starts again, and so the chain goes on. It is a chain of life – UNLESS YOU BREAK IT.

In fact the whole business of smoking is like wearing tight shoes just to obtain the pleasure you feel when you take them off. The reason that smokers cannot see it that way is twofold.

1   There is no physical pain that we can identify. It is just a feeling.
2   It happens in reverse. This is why all drugs are difficult to kick. It
    is when you are not smoking that you suffer the feeling – you do
    not blame the cigarette. When you light up you obtain relief – so
    you are fooled into believing the cigarette is some sort of pleasure
    or prop.

It may be as well to dispel some of the illusions about smoking at this
point. "The habit" doesn't exist. We have all sorts of habits during life,
some of them are very enjoyable. With a habit that tastes awful, kills
us, costs us a fortune, that we regard as filthy and disgusting and which
we would like to be free of anyway, it should be ridiculously easy to
break. Therefore why do we find it so difficult? The answer is it is not
habit but drug addiction. We have to force ourselves to learn to cope
with it. Before we know it, we are not only buying them regularly, but,
we *have* to have them. If we don't, panic sets in and, as we go through
life, we tend to smoke more and more.

This is because, like any other drug, the body tends to become
immune to the effects of nicotine and our intake tends to increase
during our lives. After quite a short period of smoking the cigarette
ceases to completely relieve the withdrawal pangs that it creates so
that when you light up a cigarette you feel better than you did a
moment before, but you are in fact more nervous and less relaxed than
you would be as a non-smoker, even when you are actually smoking the
cigarette.

So in fact the practice is even more ridiculous than wearing tight
shoes because as you go through life an increasing amount of the pain
remains even when the shoes are removed.

The position is even worse because, once the cigarette is extinguished, the nicotine rapidly begins to leave the body, which
explains why, in stress situations, the smoker tends to chain smoke.

As I said "the habit" doesn't exist. The real reason that every smoker
goes on smoking is because of that little monster inside his stomach.
Every now and again he has to feed it. The smoker himself will decide
when he does that and it tends to be on four types of occasions or a combination of them. They are:

1   Stressful situations.
2   Concentration situations.
3   Boredom situations.
4   Relaxation situations.

I will deal with each of these in a later chapter.

Apart from being a drug, nicotine is also a powerful poison and is used in insecticides (look it up in your dictionary). The nicotine content of just one cigarette, if injected directly into a vein, would kill you. In fact tobacco contains many poisons including carbon monoxide.

In case you have visions of switching to a pipe or to cigars, I would make it quite clear that the contents of this book applies to all tobacco.

The human body is the most sophisticated object on our planet. No species, the lowest amoeba or worm will survive without knowing the difference between food and poison.

Through a process of natural selection over thousands of years, our minds and bodies have developed techniques for distinguishing between food and poison and failsafe methods for ejecting the latter.

All human beings are averse to the smell and taste of tobacco until they become hooked themselves. If you blow diluted tobacco into the face of any animal or child before it becomes hooked itself, it will cough and splutter.

When we smoked that first cigarette, if we tried to inhale, it resulted in a coughing fit, or if we smoked too many the first time, we experienced a dizzy feeling or actual physical sickness. It was our bodies telling us "YOU ARE FEEDING ME POISON. STOP DOING IT". This is the stage that often decides whether we become smokers or not. It is a fallacy that physically weak and mentally weak-willed people become smokers. In fact the true tendency is just the reverse. The lucky ones are those that find that first cigarette so repulsive; physically their lungs cannot cope with it and they are cured for life. Or alternatively, they are not mentally prepared to go through the severe learning process of trying to inhale without coughing, or looking tough or sophisticated.

To me this is the most tragic part of this whole business. How hard we worked to become hooked, and this is why it is difficult to stop teenagers. Because they are still learning to smoke, because they still find cigarettes distasteful, they believe they can stop whenever they want to. Why do they not learn from us? Then again why did we not learn from our parents?

Many smokers believe they enjoy the taste and smell of the tobacco. It is an illusion.

What we are actually doing when we learn to smoke is teaching our bodies to become immune to the bad smell and taste in order to get our fix. It is similar to heroin addicts who think that they enjoy injecting themselves. The withdrawal pangs from heroin are very severe

18

and all they are really enjoying is the ritual of relieving those pangs.

The smoker teaches himself to shut his mind to the bad taste and smell to get his "fix". Ask a smoker who believes he only smokes because he enjoys the taste and smell of tobacco – "If you cannot get your normal brand of cigarette and can only obtain a brand you find distasteful, do you stop smoking?" No way, a smoker will smoke old rope rather than abstain and it doesn't matter if you switch to roll-ups, mentholated cigarettes, cigars or a pipe, to begin with they taste awful but if you persevere you will learn to like them. Smokers will even try to keep smoking during colds, 'flu, sore throats even bronchitis or emphysema.

Enjoyment has nothing to do with it. If it did, no one would smoke more than one cigarette. There are even thousands of ex-smokers hooked on that filthy nicotine chewing gum that doctors prescribe, and many of them are still smoking.

During my consultations some smokers find it alarming to realise they are drug addicts and think it will make it even more difficult to stop. In fact it is all good news for two important reasons:

1 The reason that most of us carry on smoking is because, although we know the disadvantages outweigh the advantages, we do believe that there is something in the cigarette that we actually enjoy or is some sort of prop. We feel that, after we stop smoking, there will be a void. That certain situations in our life will never be quite the same. This is an illusion. The fact is the cigarette gives nothing; it only takes away and then partially restores to create the illusion. I will explain this in more detail in a later chapter.

2 Although it is the worlds most powerful drug in the speed in which you become hooked, you are never badly hooked. Because it is a quick acting drug, it takes only three weeks for 99% of the nicotine to leave your body and the actual withdrawal pangs are so mild that most smokers have lived and died without ever realising that they suffer them.

You will quite rightly ask why it is that smokers find it so difficult to stop, can go through months of torture and many can go through the rest of their lives at odd times pining for a cigarette? The answer is the second reason why we smoke – The Brainwashing. The chemical addiction is easy to cope with.

Most smokers go all night without a cigarette, the withdrawal pangs do not even wake them up.

19

Many smokers will actually leave the bedroom before they light that first cigarette, many will have breakfast first, many will wait until they arrive at work. They can suffer ten hours withdrawal pangs and it doesn't even bother them, but if they went 10 hours during the day without one, they'd be tearing their hair out.

Many smokers will buy a new car nowadays and refrain from smoking in it. Many will visit theatres, supermarkets, churches etc and it doesn't bother them not being able to smoke. Even on the tube trains there have been no riots. Smokers are almost pleased for someone or something to enforce them to stop smoking.

Nowadays many smokers will automatically refrain from smoking in the home of, or merely in the company of, non-smokers with little discomfort to themselves. In fact most smokers have extended periods during which they abstain without effort. Even in my case I would quite happily relax all evening without a cigarette. In the later years as a smoker, I actually used to look forward to the evenings when I could stop choking myself (what a ridiculous habit).

The chemical addiction is easy to cope with (even when you are still addicted) and there are thousands of smokers that remain casual smokers all their lives. They are just as heavily addicted as the heavy smoker. There are even heavy smokers that have kicked the habit but will have an occasional cigar and that keeps them addicted.

As I say the actual nicotine addiction is not the main problem. It just acts like a catalyst to keep our minds confused over the real problem. The Brainwashing.

It may be of consolation to lifelong and heavy smokers to know that it is just as easy for them to stop as casual smokers. In a peculiar way it is easier. The further you go along the habit the more it drags you down and the greater the gain when you stop.

It may be of further consolation for you to know that the rumours that occasionally circulate e.g. "It takes seven years for the 'gunge' to leave your body" or "every cigarette you smoke takes five minutes off your life" – are untrue.

Do not think the bad health effects of smoking are exaggerated. If anything they are sadly understated, but the truth is the "five minutes" rule is obviously an estimation and only applies if you contract one of the killer diseases or just "gunge" yourself to a standstill.

In fact the "gunge" never leaves your body completely. If there are smokers about, it is in the atmosphere and even non-smokers acquire a small percentage. However these bodies of ours are incredible machines, and have enormous powers of recovery, providing you haven't already triggered-off one of the irreversible diseases. If you stop now your body will recover within a matter of a few weeks, almost to the point that you had never been a smoker.

As I have said it is never too late to stop. I have helped to cure many smokers in their 50s and 60s and even a few in their 70s. The further it drags you down the greater the relief. When I finally stopped I went straight from 100 a day to ZERO, and didn't have one bad pang. In fact, it was actually enjoyable, even during the withdrawal period.

But we *must* remove "the brainwashing".

7

Brainwashing and the Sleeping Partner

How or why do we start smoking in the first place? To fully understand this you need to examine the powerful effect of the subconscious mind, or, as I call it "the sleeping partner".

We all tend to think we are intelligent, dominant human beings deciding our paths through life. In fact 99 per cent of our make-up is moulded. We are just a product of the society that we are brought up in. The sort of clothes we wear, the houses we live in, our basic life patterns. Even on those matters on which we tend to differ e.g. Labour or Conservative Governments. It is not coincidence that the former tends to come from the working classes and the latter from the middle and upper classes. The subconscious is an extremely powerful influence in our lives and even in matters of fact rather than opinion, millions of people can be deluded. Before Columbus sailed round the world the majority of people knew it to be flat. Today we know it is round. If I wrote a dozen books trying to persuade you that it was flat I could not do it, and yet, how many of us have been into space to see the ball? Even if you have flown or sailed round the world, how do you know that you were not travelling in a circle above a flat surface?

Advertising men know well the power of suggestion on the subconscious mind. Thus the large posters the smoker is hit with as he drives around, the adverts in every magazine. You think that's a waste of money, that it would not persuade you to buy cigarettes? You are wrong! Try it out for yourself. Next time you go into a pub or restaurant on a cold day and your companion asks you what you are having to drink, instead of saying just a Brandy (or whatever) embellish it with "Do you know what I would really enjoy today? That marvellous warm glow of a Brandy". You will find that people that even dislike Brandy will join you.

From our earliest recollections our subconscious minds are being bombarded daily with information telling us that cigarettes relax us, give us confidence, courage and that the most precious thing on this earth is a cigarette. You think that I exaggerate? Whenever you see a cartoon or film or play with someone about to be executed or shot, what is their last request. That's right, a cigarette. The impact of this does not register on our conscious minds but the sleeping partner has time to absorb it. What the message is really saying is "The most precious thing on this earth, my last thought and action will be the smoking of a cigarette. In every war film the injured man is given a cigarette.

You think that it is different nowadays? No, in just the same way our children are being bombarded with these large hoardings and magazine adverts. Cigarette advertising is supposed to be banned on television nowadays and yet in peak viewing hours the worlds' top snooker players and darts players are seen constantly puffing away. The programmes are usually sponsored by the tobacco giants and this is the most sinister trend of all in today's advertising, the link with sporting occasions and the jet set. Grand Prix racing cars modelled and even named after cigarette brand names or is it the other way round? There are even "plugs" on television nowadays depicting a naked couple sharing a cigarette in bed after having sex. The implications are obvious. How my admiration goes out to the advertisers of the small cigar, not for their motives, but for the brilliance of their campaign, whereby a man is about to face death or disaster, usually his balloon is on fire and about to crash, or the sidecar of a motorbike is about to crash into a river or he is Columbus and his ship is about to go over the edge of the world. Not a word is spoken, soft music plays, he lights up a cigar; a look of sheer bliss covers his face. The conscious mind might not realise that the smoker is even watching the advert, but the "sleeping partner" is patiently digesting the obvious implications.

True there is publicity the other way. The cancer scares, the legs being amputated, the bad breath campaigns, but these do not actually stop people smoking. Logically they should do but the fact is they do not. They do not even prevent youngsters from starting. All the years that I remained a smoker, I honestly believed that had I known of the links between lung cancer and cigarette smoking, I would never have become a smoker. The truth is that it doesn't make the slightest bit of difference. The trap is the same today as when Sir Walter Raleigh fell into it. All the anti-smoking campaigns just help to add to the confusion. Even the products themselves, those lovely shining packets that lure you to engulf their contents, contain a deadly warning on their sides. What smoker ever reads it, let alone brings himself to face the consequences of it.

I believe that a leading cigarette manufacturer is actually using the

Government Health Warning to sell their products. Many of their scenes include frightening features such as spiders, dragonflies and the Venus flytrap. The Health Warning is now so large and bold, the smoker, however hard he tries, cannot avoid it. The pang of fear which the smoker suffers causes an association of ideas with the glossy gold packet.

Ironically the most powerful force in this brainwashing is the smoker himself. It is a fallacy that smokers are weak-willed and physically weak specimens. You have to be physically strong in order to cope with the poison.

This is one of the reasons why smokers refuse to accept the overwhelming statistics that smoking cripples your health. Everyone knows of an Uncle Fred who smoked 40 a day, never had a day's illness in his life, and lived to 80. They refuse to even consider the hundreds of other smokers who are cut down in their prime or the fact that Uncle Fred might still be alive if he hadn't been a smoker.

If you do a small survey amongst your friends and colleagues, you will find that most smokers are in fact strong-willed people. They tend to be self-employed, business executives and certain specialised professions such as Doctors, Lawyers, Policemen, Teachers, Salesmen, Nurses, Secretaries, Housewives with children etc. In other words, anybody leading a stressful existence. The main delusion of smokers is that smoking relieves stress and tends to be associated with the dominant type; the type that takes on responsibility and stress that falls for the illusion; and, of course, they are the types that we admire and therefore tend to copy. The other group that tends to get hooked are the people in monotonous jobs because the other main reason for smoking is boredom. Also an illusion I am afraid.

The extent of the brainwashing is quite incredible. As a society we get all uptight about glue-sniffing, heroin addiction, etc.

The actual deaths from glue-sniffing do not amount to ten and deaths from heroin are less than a hundred a year in this country.

There is another drug – nicotine – over 60 per cent of us have become hooked in our lives and the majority spend the rest of their lives paying through the nose. Most of their spare money goes on cigarettes and hundreds of thousands of people have their lives ruined every year because they became hooked. It is the No. 1 killer disease in western society including road accidents, fires, etc.

Why is it that we regard glue-sniffing, heroin addiction, etc., as such a great evil whereas the drug that we spend most of our money on and which is actually killing us, we used to regard a few years ago as a perfectly acceptable sociable habit? In recent years it is regarded as a

24

slightly unsociable habit that may injure our health and is not only legal, but on sale in glossy packets in every newsagents, pub, club, garage, restaurant, and the biggest vested interest is our own government. They make £5,000,000,000 per year and the tobacco companies spend £100,000,000 per year in promotion alone.

You need to start building a sales resistance to this brainwashing. Just as if you were buying a car from a secondhand dealer, you would be nodding politely but you would not believe a word the man was saying.

Start looking behind these glossy packets at the filth and poison beneath. Do not be fooled by the cut glass ashtrays or the gold lighter or the millions who have been conned. Start asking yourself

Why am I doing it?
Do I really need to?

NO OF COURSE YOU DON'T.

I find this brainwashing aspect the most difficult of all to explain. Why is it that an otherwise rational, intelligent human being becomes a complete imbecile about his own addiction. It pains me to confess that out of the thousands of people that I have assisted in kicking the habit, I was the biggest idiot of all.

Not only did I reach a hundred a day myself but my father was a heavy smoker. He was a strong man, cut down in his prime due to smoking. I can remember watching him when I was a boy, he would be coughing and spluttering in the mornings. I could see he wasn't enjoying it and it was so obvious to me that something evil had got possession of him. I can remember saying to my mother – *"Don't ever let me become a smoker."*

At the age of 15 I was a physical fitness fanatic. Sport was my life and I was full of courage and confidence. If anybody had said to me in those days that I would end up smoking 100 cigarettes a day, I would have gambled my lifetime's earnings that it would not happen and I would have given any odds that had been asked.

At the age of 40 I was a physical and mental cigarette "junky". I had reached the stage where I couldn't carry out the most mundane physical or mental act without first lighting up. With most smokers it's the normal stresses of life, like answering the telephone or when socialising. I couldn't even change a television programme or a light bulb without lighting up.

I knew it was killing me, there was no way I could kid myse wise; but why I couldn't see what it was doing to me mentally, understand. It was almost jumping up and biting me on the r

25

ridiculous thing was most smokers suffer the illusion at some time in their life that they enjoy a cigarette. I never ever suffered that illusion. I smoked because I thought it helped me to concentrate and because it helped my nerves, etc. Now I am a non-smoker the most difficult part is trying to believe that those days actually happened. It's like awakening from a nightmare and that is about the size of it. It's a drug, all your senses are drugged – your taste buds – your sense of smell and the worst aspects of smoking isn't the injury to your health or pocket, it is the warping of the mind. All you search for is any justifiable excuse to go on smoking and put blinkers on about the other aspects.

I remember at one stage switching to a pipe after a failed attempt to kick cigarettes in the belief that it was less harmful and would cut down my intake.

Some of those pipe tobaccos are absolutely foul. The aroma can be pleasant but, to start with, they are awful to smoke. I can remember that for about three months the tip of my tongue was as sore as a boil. A liquid brown goo collects in the bottom of the bowl of the pipe. Occasionally you unwittingly bring the bowl above the horizontal and before you realise it you have swallowed a mouthful of the filthy stuff. The result is usually to immediately throw up, no matter what company you are in.

It took me three months to learn to cope with the pipe, but what I cannot understand is why I didn't sit down sometime during that three months and ask myself why I was submitting myself to the torture.

Of course once you learn to cope with the pipe, no one appears more contented than the pipe smoker and most of them are convinced that they smoke because they enjoy the pipe. But why did they have to work so hard to learn to like it when they were perfectly happy without it?

The answer is, once you have become addicted to nicotine, the brainwashing is increased. Your subconscious mind knows that the little monster has to be fed and you block your mind from everything else. As I have already stated it is fear that keeps people smoking. The fear of that empty insecure feeling that you get when you stop supplying nicotine. Because you are not aware of it doesn't mean it isn't there. You don't have to understand it any more than a cat needs to understand where the under-floor hot-water pipes are, it just knows that if it sits in that position it gets the feeling of warmth.

It is the brainwashing that is the main difficulty in giving up smoking. The brainwashing from the upbringing of our society reinforced with the brainwashing from our own addiction and the most powerful effect of all, the brainwashing of our friends, relatives and colleagues.

The only thing that gets us onto it in the first place is all the other people doing it. We feel we are missing out. We work so hard to become hooked and yet nobody ever finds out what they have been missing. But every time we see another smoker he reassures us that there must be something in it otherwise he wouldn't be doing it. Even when we have kicked the habit it is usually a party, Xmas or other social functions, a smoker will light up, the ex-smoker feels he is being deprived. He feels safe he can have just one and, before he knows it, he is hooked again.

This brainwashing is very powerful and you need to be aware of its effects. Many older smokers will remember the "Paul Temple" detective series that was a very popular radio programme after the war. One of the series was dealing with drug addiction, namely Marijuana commonly known as "Pot" or "Grass". Unbeknown to the smoker, wicked men were selling cigarettes which contained "Pot". There were no harmful effects, you merely became addicted and had to go on buying these cigarettes. During my recent consultations literally hundreds of smokers have admitted to trying "Pot". None of them said they became hooked on it. I was about seven years old when I listened to the programme. It was my first knowledge of drug addiction. The concept of "addiction", being compelled to go on taking the drug, filled me with horror and, even to this day, in spite of the fact that I am fairly convinced that "Pot" is not addictive, I would not dare take one puff of Marijuana. How ironic that I should have ended up a chronic junky on the world's No. 1 addictive drug. If only Paul Temple had warned me about the cigarette itself. How even more ironic that over 40 years later mankind spends thousands of pounds on cancer research and yet millions of pounds are spent persuading healthy teenagers to become hooked on the filthy weed, our own government having the largest, vested interest.

We are about to remove the brainwashing. It is not the non-smoker that is being deprived but the poor smoker who is being deprived of a lifetime of:

HEALTH
ENERGY
WEALTH
PEACE OF MIND
CONFIDENCE
COURAGE
SELF-RESPECT
HAPPINESS.

And what does he gain from these considerable sacrifices?

ABSOLUTELY NOTHING!

JUST THE ILLUSION OF TRYING TO GET BACK TO THE STATE OF PEACE, TRANQUILLITY AND CONFIDENCE THAT THE NON-SMOKER ENJOYS ALL THE TIME.

8

Relieving Withdrawal Pangs

As I explained earlier, smokers think they smoke because of enjoyment, relaxation or for some sort of boost. In fact this is an illusion, the actual reason is the relief of withdrawal pangs.

In the early days we used the cigarette as a social prop. We can take it or leave it. However the subtle chain has started, our subconscious mind begins to learn that a cigarette taken at certain times tends to be pleasurable.

The more we become hooked on the drug the greater the relief of the withdrawal pangs and therefore the further the cigarette drags you down and the more you are fooled into believing it is doing the opposite. It all happens so slowly, so gradually, you are not even aware that it is happening. Each day you feel no different to the day before. Most smokers don't even realise they are hooked until they actually try to stop and even then many won't admit to it. A few stalwarts just keep their heads in the sand all their lives, trying to convince themselves and other people that they enjoy it.

I have had the following conversation with hundreds of teenagers.

ME: You realise it is a drug and that the only reason you are smoking is that you cannot stop.
  T: Nonsense! I enjoy it. If I didn't I would stop.
ME: Just stop for a week to prove to me you can if you want to.
  T: No need, I enjoy it, if I wanted to stop I would.
ME: Just stop for a week to prove to yourself you are not hooked.
  T: What's the point – I enjoy it.

As already stated, smokers tend to relieve their withdrawal pangs either at times of stress, boredom, concentration, relaxation or a combination of these factors. This is explained in greater detail in the next few chapters.

9

The Stress Situation

I am not only referring to the great tragedies of life but also the minor stresses, the socialising, the telephone call, the housewife with noisy, young children, etc.

Let us use the telephone conversation as an example. For most people the telephone is slightly stressful, particularly for the business man. Most calls aren't a satisfied customer or your boss congratulating you, it's usually some sort of aggro – something going wrong or somebody wants money etc. At that time the smoker, if he isn't already doing so, will light up a cigarette. He doesn't know why he does this but he does know that, for some reason, it appears to help.

What has actually happened is this. Without being conscious of it, he has already been suffering aggravation i.e. the withdrawal pangs. By partially relieving that aggravation at the same time as normal stress, the total stress is reduced and the smoker gets a boost. At this point the boost is not, in fact, an illusion. The smoker will feel better than before he lit the cigarette. However, it is, in fact, an illusion because, even when smoking that cigarette, the smoker is more tense than if he were a non-smoker, because the more you go into the drug, the more it knocks you down and the less it restores you when you smoke.

I promised no shock treatment. In the example I am about to give, I am not trying to shock you, I am merely emphasising that cigarettes destroy your nerves not relax them.

Try to imagine getting to the stage where a doctor tells you that unless you stop smoking he is going to have to remove your legs. Just for a moment pause and try to visualise life without your legs. Try to imagine the frame of mind of a man that, issued with that warning, actually continuing smoking and then having his legs removed.

I used to hear stories like that and dismissed them as cranks. In fact I used to wish a doctor would tell me that, then I would have stopped. Yet I was already one of these cranks fully expecting any day to have a brain haemorrhage and not only lose my legs but my life. I didn't think of myself as a crank, just a heavy smoker.

Those people aren't cranks. This is what this awful drug does to you.

As you go through life it systematically takes away your nerve and courage. The more it takes your courage away, the more you are deluded into believing the cigarette is doing the opposite. We have all heard of the panic feeling that smokers get when they are out late at night and in fear of running out of cigarettes. Non-smokers do not suffer it, the cigarette causes that feeling. At the same time as you go through life the cigarette not only destroys your nerves but is a powerful poison, progressively destroying your physical health. By the time the smoker reaches the stage that it is killing him physically, he believes the cigarette is his courage and, at that time in life, he thinks he most needs it and cannot face life without it.

Get it clear into your head that that cigarette is not relieving your nerves; it is slowly but steadily destroying them and one of the great positive gains from breaking the habit is the return of your confidence and self-assurance.

10

The Boring Situation

If you are already smoking at this moment you will probably have already forgotten about it until I reminded you.

Another fallacy about smoking is that cigarettes relieve boredom. Boredom is a frame of mind and when you smoke a cigarette your mind isn't saying "I'm smoking a cigarette, I'm smoking a cigarette". The only time that happens is, when you have been deprived for a long time, or when you are trying to cut down, or those first few cigarettes after a failed attempt to stop.

The true situation is this; when you are addicted to nicotine and are not smoking, there is something missing. If you have something to occupy your mind that isn't stressful, you can go for long periods without it bothering you. However, when you are bored there's nothing to take your mind off it and so you feed the monster. When you are indulging yourself (i.e. not trying to stop or cut down), even the lighting up becomes subconscious. Even pipe smokers and roll-your-own smokers can perform this ritual automatically. If any smoker tries to remember the cigarettes he has smoked during the day, he can only remember a small proportion of them e.g. the first of the day or the one after a meal.

The truth is that cigarettes indirectly tend to increase boredom, because they make you feel lethargic and instead of undertaking some energetic activity, smokers tend to lounge around bored, relieving their withdrawal pangs.

11

The Concentration Situation

Again cigarettes do not help concentration, it is just an illusion. It tends to be writers, artists or other professions involving inspiration and mental activity that smoke for this reason.

When you are trying to concentrate, you automatically try to avoid aggravations like feeling cold or too hot or other distractions. The smoker is already suffering an aggravation from that little monster wanting his fix. So when he wants to concentrate, he doesn't even have to think about it, he automatically lights up partially ending the craving, gets on with the matter in hand, and has already forgotten that he is smoking.

Cigarettes do not help concentration, they help to ruin it, because, after a while, even when smoking the cigarette, the withdrawal pangs cease to be completely relieved. The smoker then increases the intake and the problem then increases. It is a snowball to disaster.

12

The Relaxing Situation

Most smokers think the cigarette helps to relax them. The truth is nicotine is actually a chemical stimulant. If you take your pulse and then smoke two consecutive cigarettes, there will be a marked increase in your pulse rate.

One of the favourite cigarettes for most smokers is the one after a meal. The meal is the time of day when we stop working, we sit down and relax, we relieve our hunger and thirst and are then completely relaxed and satisfied. However the poor smoker cannot relax as he has another hunger to satisfy. He thinks of it as the icing on the cake, in fact it is just the little monster needs feeding.

The truth is the nicotine addict can never be completely relaxed and, as you go through life, the worse it gets.

The most un-relaxed people on this planet aren't non-smokers but the 50 year old business executives, chain smoking, permanently coughing and spluttering, having high blood pressure, constantly irritable. At this point cigarettes can cease to even partially relieve the symptoms that they have created.

The whole business of smoking can be likened to a fly being caught in a pitcher plant. To begin with the fly is eating the nectar, at some imperceptible stage the plant begins to eat the fly.

Isn't it time you climbed out of that plant?

13

Combination Cigarettes

No a combination cigarette is not when you are smoking two or more at the same time. It is when that happens to you that you begin to wonder why you were smoking the first one. I once burnt the back of my hand trying to put a cigarette in my mouth when there was already one there. Actually it is not quite as stupid as you think. As I have already said, eventually the cigarette ceases to relieve the withdrawal pangs and even when you are smoking the cigarette there is still something missing. This is the terrible frustration of the chain smoker. Whenever you need the boost, you are already smoking and this is why heavy smokers turn to drink or other drugs, but I digress.

A combination cigarette is one occasioned by 2 or more of our usual reasons for smoking e.g. Social functions, Parties, Weddings, Meals in restaurants. These are examples of occasions that are both stressful and relaxing. This might at first appear to be a contradiction but it isn't. Any form of socialising can be stressful. Even with your friends there is the normal banter and repartee and at the same time you want to be enjoying yourself and be completely relaxed.

The worst situations are the triple combinations such as a game of cards. There you have the stress from gambling, the concentration in the game and at the same time it's your leisure and you want to be completely relaxed. During a game of cards no matter how slight the withdrawal pangs are, all smokers will be chain smoking, even otherwise casual smokers. The ashtrays will fill and overflow in no time. There will a constant fall out cloud above head height. If you were to tap any of the smokers on the shoulder and ask them if they were enjoying it, the answer would be "You have got to be joking". It is often after nights like that, when we wake up with a throat like a cess pit, that we decide to stop smoking.

These combination cigarettes are often special ones, the ones that when we are contemplating giving-up smoking, we think that life will never be quite as enjoyable again. In fact it is the same principle, it is just the relief of withdrawl pangs and at certain times we have greater need to relieve them than others.

Let us make it quite clear. It is not the cigarette that is special, it is the occasion. Once we have removed the need for the cigarette, those occasions will become more enjoyable and the stress situation less stressful. This will be explained in great detail in the next chapter.

14

What am I Giving Up?

ABSOLUTELY NOTHING! The thing that makes it difficult for us to give up is fear. The fear that we are being deprived of our pleasure or prop. The fear that certain pleasant situations will never be quite the same again or the fear of being unable to cope with stressful situations.

In other words the effect of the brainwashing is to delude us into believing that there is a weakness in us or something inherent in the cigarette that we need and that when we stop smoking there will be a void.

Get it clearly in your mind, CIGARETTES DO NOT FILL A VOID. THEY CREATE IT!

These bodies of ours are the most sophisticated objects on this planet. Whether you believe in a creator, a process of natural selection or a combination of both. Whatever being or system devised these bodies of ours, it is a thousand times more effective than man! Man cannot create the smallest living cell, let alone the miracle of eyesight, reproduction our circulatory system or our brains. If the creator or process had intended us to smoke we would have been provided with some filter device to keep the poisons out of our bodies and some sort of chimney.

Our bodies are in fact provided with failsafe warning devices in the form of the cough, the dizziness, the sickness etc. and we ignore these at our peril.

The beautiful truth is – there is nothing to give up. Once you purge that little monster from your body and the brainwashing from your mind, you will neither want cigarettes or need them.

Cigarettes do not improve meals, they ruin them. They destroy your sense of taste and smell. Observe smokers in a restaurant, smoking between courses. It is not the meal that they are enjoying, in fact they cannot wait for the meal to be over, the meal is interfering with the cigarette. Many of them do it in spite of the fact that they know it causes offence to non-smokers. It is not that smokers are generally inconsiderate people, it is just that they are so miserable without the cigarette. They are between the devil and the deep blue sea. They either have to abstain and be miserable because they cannot smoke, or smoke and still be miserable because they are offending other people and feel guilty and despise themselves because of it.

Watch smokers at an official function, where they have to wait for "The royal toast" – many of them develop weak bladders and have to sneak off for the crafty puff, that is when you see smoking for the true addiction that it is. Smokers do not smoke because they enjoy it, it's because they are miserable without it.

Because many of us start smoking on social occasions when we are young and shy we have this belief that we cannot enjoy social occasions without a cigarette. This is nonsense. Tobacco takes away your confidence. In fact the greatest evidence of the fear that cigarettes install in smokers is not that they cause cancer and other horrendous diseases (the smoker appears to be oblivious to that fact), but their effect on women. Practically all women are fastidious about their personal appearance. They wouldn't dream of appearing at a social function not immaculately turned out and smelling beautifully. Yet knowing that their breath smells like a stale ashtray does not seem to deter them in the least. I know that it bothers them greatly, many hate the smell of their own hair and clothes yet it doesn't deter them. Such is the fears that this awful drug instils in the smoker.

Cigarettes do not help social occasions, they destroy them; having to hold a drink in one hand and a cigarette in the other; trying to dispose of the ash and the continual chain of dogends; trying not to breathe smoke and fumes into the face of the person you are conversing with; wondering whether they can smell your breath or see the stains on your teeth.

Not only is there nothing to give up, but there are marvellous positive gains. When smokers contemplate giving-up smoking they tend to concentrate on health, money and social stigma. These are obviously valid and important but I personally believe the greatest gains from giving up are mental and for varying reasons they include:

1 The return of your confidence and courage.
2 Freedom from the slavery.
3 Not to have to go through life suffering the awful black shadows at the back of your mind, knowing you are being despised by half of the population and worst of all despising yourself.

In fact not only is life better as a non-smoker it is infinitely more so. I do not only mean you will be healthier and wealthier, I mean you will be happier and enjoy life far more.

The marvellous gains from being a non-smoker are discussed in the next few chapters.

Some smokers find it difficult to appreciate this "Void" concept and the following analogy may assist you.

Imagine having a small sore on your hand. I notice it and recommend a marvellous ointment. You apply the ointment and the sore disappears immediately. A month later the sore re-appears, larger and more painful. You apply the ointment again and it immediately disappears again. This process continues until the sore is the size of your hand and is now burning with pain. By now you will be getting extremely worried. Although the miracle ointment removes the sore you are wondering where it will all end up. Will the sore eventually spread over your whole body? You go to your doctor, he cannot help you. You try other remedies – nothing helps, only this marvellous ointment. You then discover that this marvellous ointment doesn't in fact cure the sore. It merely takes it beneath the surface of the skin and the sore is actually feeding on the ointment, that it is the ointment that is causing the sore to grow and that if you stop using it the sore will heal permanently in its own good time.

Would you carry on using the ointment?
Would it take willpower not to use it?
Would you be miserable about it?

Of course not, you would be both relieved and delighted that you had found the cause of the evil. The analogy is the same with the cigarette and in the case of the cigarette there should be even greater rejoicing. The equivalent of the sore isn't the dreadful health risks, or the fortune you spend on them (they are greater reasons for stopping), the sore is the withdrawal pangs, the feeling of depression and insecurity. The cigarette is causing them not relieving them.

STOP PUNISHING YOURSELF.

15

Self-Imposed Slavery

Usually when smokers try to stop the main reasons are health, money, and social stigma. Part of the brainwashing of this awful drug is the sheer slavery.

Man fought hard in the last century to abolish slavery and yet the smoker spends his life suffering self-imposed slavery. He seems to be oblivious to the fact that, when he is allowed to smoke, he wishes that he were a non-smoker. With most of the cigarettes we smoke in our lives, not only do we not enjoy them, but we aren't even aware that we are smoking them. It is only after a period of abstinence that we actually suffer the delusion of enjoying a cigarette e.g. the first in the morning, the one after a meal etc.

The only time that the cigarette becomes precious is when we ourselves are trying to cut down or abstain, or when society tries to enforce us to e.g. when attending churches, hospitals, supermarkets, theatres etc. etc.

The confirmed smoker should bear in mind that this trend will get worse and worse. Today it is tube trains – tomorrow it will be all public places.

Gone are the days when the smoker could enter a friend's or stranger's house and say, "Do you mind if I smoke?" Nowadays the poor smoker, on entering a strange house, will search desperately for an ashtray and hope to find dogends in it. If there is no ashtray he will generally try to last out and, if he cannot, he will ask for permission to smoke and is just as likely to be told:

"Smoke if you have to."

or "Well, we would rather you didn't. The smell seems to linger so."

The poor smoker, who was already feeling wretched, wants the ground to open up and swallow him.

I remember during my smoking days every time I went to church, even during my own daughter's wedding, I should have been standing there a proud father. What was I doing? I was just thinking "Let's get on with it, so that we can get outside and have a drag."

It will help you to observe smokers on these occasions. They huddle together. It is never just one packet. There are 20 packets being thrust about and the conversation is always the same.

"Do you smoke?"

"Yes, but have one of mine."

"I will have one of yours later."

We light up and take a deep drag thinking, "Aren't we lucky, we have got our little reward, the poor non-smoker hasn't got a reward."

The poor non-smoker doesn't need a reward. We were not designed to go through life systematically poisoning our own bodies and the pathetic thing is that even when smoking the cigarette, the smoker doesn't achieve the feeling of peace, confidence and tranquillity that the non-smoker has experienced for the whole of his non-smoking life. The non-smoker wasn't sitting in the church feeling agitated and wishing his life away, he can enjoy the whole of his life.

I can also remember playing indoor bowls in the winter and pretending to have a weak bladder in order to nip off for a crafty puff. No, this wasn't a 14-year-old schoolboy but a 40-year-old Chartered Accountant. How pathetic, and even when I was back playing the game I wasn't enjoying it. I was looking forward to the finish so that I could smoke again and this was supposed to be my way of relaxing and enjoying my favourite hobby.

To me one of the tremendous joys of being a non-smoker is to be freed from that slavery and to be able to enjoy the whole of your life and not spend half of it craving for a cigarette and then, when you light up, wishing you didn't have to do it.

Smokers should bear in mind that when they are in the houses of non-smokers or even in the company of non-smokers, it is not the self-righteous non-smoker that is depriving them but the "little monster".

16

I'll Save £X a Week

I cannot repeat too often that it is brainwashing that makes it difficult to stop smoking, and the more brainwashing we can dispel before we start, the easier you will find it to achieve your goal.

Occasionally I get into arguments with what I call confirmed smokers. By my definition a confirmed smoker is somebody that can afford it, that doesn't believe it injures his health and isn't worried about the social stigma. (There are not many about nowadays.)

If it is a young man I say to him. "I cannot believe you are not worried about the money you are spending."

Usually his eyes light up. If I had attacked him on health grounds or on the social stigma he would feel at a disadvantage, but on money –

"Oh, I can afford it. It is only £X per week and I think it is worth it. It is my only vice or pleasure," etc. etc.

If it is a 20 per day smoker I say to him.

"I still cannot believe you are not worried about the money. You are going to spend about £25,000 in your lifetime. What will you do with that money, you are not even setting light to it or throwing it away. You are actually using that money to ruin your physical health, to destroy your nerves and confidence, to suffer a lifetime of slavery, a lifetime of bad breath, stained teeth, etc. Surely that must worry you?"

It is apparent at this point particularly with young smokers, that they have never considered it as a lifetime expense. For most smokers the price of a packet is bad enough. Occasionally we work out what we spend in a week, and that is bad enough. Very occasionally (and only when we think about stopping) we estimate what we spend in a year and that is frightening, but over a lifetime – it is unthinkable.

However, because it is an argument, the confirmed smoker will say:

"I can afford it. It is only so much a week." He does an "Encyclopaedia salesman" on himself.

I then say:

"I will make you an offer you cannot refuse. You pay me a £1,000 now and I will provide you with free cigarettes for the rest of your life."

If I were offering to take over a £25,000 mortgage for a £1,000 the smoker would have my signature on a piece of paper before I could move, and yet not one confirmed smoker (and please bear in mind I am not now talking to someone like yourself who plans to stop, I am talking to someone who has no intention of stopping), has ever taken me up on that offer. Why not?

Often in this point in my consultation, a smoker will say "Look, I am not really worried about the money aspect". If you are thinking along these lines, ask yourself why you are not worried? Why in other aspects of life you will go to a great deal of trouble to save a few pounds here and there and yet spend thousands of pounds poisoning yourself and hang the expense?

The answer to these questions is this. Every other decision that you make in your life will be the result of an analytical process of weighing up the pros and cons and arriving at a rational answer. It may be the wrong answer, but at least it will be the result of rational deducation. Whenever any smoker weighs up the pros and cons of smoking, the answer is a dozen times over:

"STOP SMOKING YOU ARE A MUG!"

Therefore all smokers are smoking, not because they want to, or because they decided to, but because they think they cannot stop. They therefore have to brainwash themselves. They have to keep their heads in the sand.

The strange thing is smokers will arrange pacts amongst themselves such as "First one to give in pays the other £50" and yet the thousands of pounds that they actually save by stopping doesn't seem to affect them. This is because they are still thinking with the brainwashed mind of the smoker.

Just take the sand out of your eyes for a moment. Smoking is a chain reaction and a chain for life. If you do not break that chain you will remain smoking for the rest of your life. Now estimate how much you think you will spend on smoking the rest of your life. The amount will obviously vary with each individual, but for the purpose of this exercise let us assume it is £10,000.

You will shortly be making the decision to smoke your final cigarette (not yet please – remember the initial instructions). All you have to do to remain a non-smoker is not to fall for the trap again i.e. do not smoke that first cigarette. If you do, that one cigarette will cost you £10,000.

If you think this is a trick way of looking at it you are still kidding yourself. Just work out how much money you would have saved if you hadn't smoked your first cigarette.

If you see the argument as factual just ask yourself how you would feel if there was a cheque from Littlewoods Pools for £10,000 on your carpet tomorrow. You'd be dancing with delight! So start dancing! You are about to start receiving that bonus and thats just one of the several marvellous gains you are about to receive.

During the withdrawal period you may be tempted to have just one final cigarette. It will help you to resist the temptation if you remind yourself it will cost you £10,000 (or whatever your estimate is)!

17

Health

This is the area where the brainwashing is the greatest. Smokers think they are aware of the health risks in fact they are not.

Even in my case when I was expecting my head to explode any moment, and honestly believed I was prepared to accept the consequences, I was still kidding myself.

If in those days I had taken a cigarette out of the packet and a red bleeper started to sound followed by a warning voice saying:

"O.K. Allen, this is the one! Fortunately you do get a warning and this is it. Up to now you have got away with it but if you smoke another cigarette your head will explode."

Do you think I would have lit that cigarette? If you are in doubt about the answer, just try walking up to a main road with busy traffic, stand on the kerb with your eyes closed and try to imagine you have the choice of either stopping smoking or walking blindfolded across the road before taking your next cigarette.

There is no doubt what the answer would be. All I had been doing is what I, and every other smoker, does all our smoking life; closing my mind and keeping my head in the sand hoping that I would wake up one morning and just not want to smoke anymore. Smokers cannot allow themselves even to think of the health risks, if they do, even the illusion of enjoying the habit goes.

This explains why the shock treatment used by the media on National Non-Smoking Days is so ineffective. It is only non-smokers that can bring themselves to watch it. It also explains why smokers, quoting that Uncle Fred who smoked 40 a day and lived until he was 80, will ignore the thousands of people that are brought down in their prime because of this poisonous weed.

About six times a week I have this conversation with smokers (usually the younger ones):

> ME: "Why do you want to stop?"
> SMOKER: "I can't afford it."

ME: "Aren't you worried about the health risks?"

SMOKER: "No, I could step under a bus tomorrow."

ME: "Would you deliberately step under a bus?"

SMOKER: "Of course not."

ME: "Do you not bother to look left and right when you cross the road?"

SMOKER: "Of course I do."

Exactly. The smoker goes to a lot of trouble not to step under a bus and the odds are hundreds of thousands to one against it happening. Yet the smoker risks the near certainty of being crippled by the weed and appears to be completely oblivious to the risks. Such is the power of the brainwashing.

I remember one famous British golfer who wouldn't go on the American circuit because he was afraid of flying. Yet he would be chain smoking round the golf course. Isn't it strange how, if we felt there was the slightest fault in an aeroplane, we wouldn't go up in it, even though the risks are hundreds of thousands against death, yet we take a one in four certainty with the cigarette and are apparently oblivious to it. And what does the smoker get out of it?

ABSOLUTELY NOTHING!!!

Another common myth about smoking is the smokers' cough. Many of the younger people that come to see me are not worried about their health because they do not cough. The true facts are just the reverse. A cough is one of nature's failsafe methods of dispelling foreign matter from the lungs. The cough itself is not a disease, it is just a symptom. When a smoker coughs it is because their lungs are trying to dispel cancer-triggering tars and poisons. When he does not cough those tars and poisons remain in the lungs, that is when they cause cancer.

Just think of it this way. If you had a nice car and allowed the rust to get in without doing anything about it, that's a pretty stupid thing to do because it will soon be a heap of rust and will not carry you about. However, it is not the end of the world, it is only money and you can always buy a new one. Your body is the vehicle that carries you through life. We all say that your health is your most valued asset, how true it is, and sick millionaires will tell you so. Most of us can look back at some illness or accident in our lives when we prayed to get better (HOW SOON WE FORGET). By being a smoker you are not only letting rust get in and doing nothing about it, you are systematically poisoning the vehicle you need to go through life, and you only get one.

Wise up, you don't have to do it, and remember it is doing ABSOLUTELY NOTHING FOR YOU.

Just for the moment take your head out of the sand and ask yourself if you know for certain that the next cigarette would be the one to trigger off cancer in your body and whether you would actually smoke it? Forget the disease, it is difficult to imagine the disease, but imagine now you have to go to the Royal Marsden to suffer those awful tests, Radium treatment etc. Now you are not planning the rest of your life. What is going to happen to your family and loved ones, your plans and dreams? You are now planning your death.

I often see the people that it happens to. They didn't think it would happen to them either, and the worst thing about it isn't the disease itself, but the knowledge they have brought it on themselves. All our lives as smokers we are saying "I'll stop tomorrow". Try to imagine how those people feel that "hit the button". For them the brainwashing is ended. They then see the habit as it really is and spend the remainder of their lives thinking "Why did I kid myself I needed to smoke? If I only had the chance to go back!"

Stop kidding yourself. You have the chance. It's a chain reaction. If you smoke the next cigarette it will lead to the next one and the next. It's already happening to you.

At the beginning of the book I promised you no shock treatment. If you have already decided you are going to stop smoking this isn't shock treatment for you. If you are still in doubt, skip the remainder of this chapter and come back to it when you have read the rest of the book.

Volumes of statistics have already been written about the damage that cigarettes can cause to the smoker's health. The trouble is that until the smoker decides to stop he doesn't want to know. Even that government health warning is a waste of time because the smoker puts blinkers on and, if he inadvertently reads it, the first thing he does is light up a cigarette.

Smokers tend to think of the health hazard as a hit and miss affair like stepping on a mine. Get it into your head, it is already happening. Every time you puff on a cigarette you are breathing cancer-triggering tars into your lungs and cancer is by no means the worst of the killer diseases that cigarettes cause or contribute to. They are also a powerful contributory cause to Heart disease, Arteriosclerosis, Emphysema, Angina, Thrombosis, Chronic Bronchitis and Asthma.

Smokers also suffer the illusion that the ill-effects of smoking are overstated. The reverse is the case. There is no doubt that cigarettes are the No. 1 cause of death in Western society. The trouble is in many cases where cigarettes cause the death or are a contributory factor, it is not blamed on cigarettes in the statistics.

It was recently published that 44 per cent of household fires are caused from cigarettes and I wonder how many road accidents have been caused by cigarettes during that split second you take your eye off the road to light up.

I am normally a careful driver but the nearest I came to death (except from smoking itself) was when trying to roll a cigarette whilst driving and I hate to think of the number of times I coughed a cigarette out of my mouth whilst driving – it always seemed to end up between the seats. I am sure many other smoking drivers have had that experience of trying to locate the burning cigarette with one hand whilst trying to drive with the other.

The effect of the brainwashing is that we tend to think like the man who, having fallen off a 100-storey building, is heard to say, as he passes the 50th floor, "So far so good!" We think that as we have got away with it so far, one more cigarette won't make the difference.

Trying to see it another way, "The Habit" is a continuous chain for life, each cigarette creating the need for the next. When you start the habit you light a fuse. The trouble is, YOU DON'T KNOW HOW LONG THE FUSE IS. Every time that you light a cigarette you are one step nearer to the "Bomb" exploding. HOW WILL YOU KNOW IF IT'S THE NEXT ONE?

18

Energy

Most smokers are aware of congesting their lungs but many are not aware of the general lethargy that smoking causes.

In addition to congesting the lungs the smoker is progressively gunging up his arteries and veins with poisons such as nicotine, carbon monoxide and others.

Our lungs and bloodstreams are intended to carry oxygen and other nutrients to the various organs and muscles of our body. The smoker is increasingly starving every muscle and organ of his body of oxygen so that they are daily functioning less efficiently and he is not only becoming more and more lethargic each day but also has less resistance to other diseases.

Because it all happens so slowly and gradually, the smoker is unaware that it is happening. Each day he feels no different from the previous day and because he doesn't feel ill, he tends to regard the permanent state of lethargy as getting old.

From being a very fit teenager I was permanently tired for 25 years. I thought it was only children and teenagers that had energy. One of the marvellous bonuses for me shortly after stopping was to suddenly have energy again. To actually want to exercise.

This abusing of the body and the lack of energy tends to lead to other abuses. The smoker tends to avoid sporting activity, other pastimes and leans towards over-eating and drinking.

19

It Relaxes and Gives Me Confidence

This is the worst fallacy of all about smoking and to me this ranks with the ending of the slavery, the greatest benefit of giving up smoking, not to have to go through life with that permanent feeling of insecurity that smokers suffer.

Smokers find it very difficult to believe that the cigarette actually causes that insecure feeling you get when you are out late at night and running out of cigarettes. Non-smokers do not suffer that feeling. It is the tobacco that causes it.

I only became aware of many of the advantages of giving up smoking months after I stopped as a result of my consultations with other smokers.

For 25 years I refused to have a medical. If I wanted life assurance I insisted on no medical and paid higher premiums as a result. I hated visiting hospitals, doctors or dentists. I couldn't face the thought of getting old and thinking about pensions and such-like.

None of these things did I relate to my smoking habit, but getting off of it has been like awaking from a bad dream. Nowadays I look forward to each day. Of course bad things happen in my life and I am subject to the normal stresses and strains, but it is so nice to have the confidence to cope with them and that extra health, energy and confidence make the good times more enjoyable too.

20

Those Sinister Black Shadows

Another of the great joys of giving up the weed is to be free of those sinister black shadows at the back of our minds.

All smokers know they are mugs and close their minds to the ill-effects of smoking. For most of our lives smoking is automatic but the black shadows are always lurking in our subsconscious minds, just beneath the surface.

Throughout our smoking lives there are moments when these black shadows are brought to the surface. When we see that Government Health Warning, a cancer scare, National Non-Smoking day, or a coughing fit, a pain in the chest or the pained look of one of our children, friends or relatives; the awareness of our bad breath and stained teeth at the dentists or when kissing or even conversing with a non-smoker. Just the mere loss of self-respect and despising oneself for being a smoker.

Even when we are not conscious of these things, those black shadows are always lurking just beneath the surface and this tug of war will get worse and worse the further you get into "the habit" and it won't end until you rid yourself of this awful addiction.

I cannot emphasise enough how marvellous it is to be finally free of those awful black shadows or the joy of knowing you do not have to smoke anymore.

The last two chapters have dealt with the considerable advantages of being a non-smoker. I feel it necessary to give a balanced account and so this next chapter lists the advantages of being a smoker.

21

The Advantages of Being a Smoker

22

The Willpower Method of Stopping

It is an accepted fact in our society that it is very difficult to give-up smoking. Even books advising you how to do so usually start off by telling you how difficult it is. The truth is it is ridiculously easy. Yes, I can understand you questioning that statement, but just consider it.

If your aim is to run a mile in under 4 minutes that's difficult. You may have to sustain years of hard training and even then you may be physically incapable of doing it. (Even much of that was in the mind. Isn't it strange how difficult it was until Bannister actually did it and nowadays it is commonplace?).

However, in order to stop smoking, all you have to do is not smoke anymore. No one forces you to smoke (apart from yourself) and unlike food or drink, you don't need to do it to survive. So if you want to stop doing it, why should it be difficult? In fact it isn't. It is only smokers that make it difficult by using the Willpower Method. I define the Willpower Method as any method whereby the smoker feels he is making some sort of sacrifice. Let us just consider the Willpower Method.

We do not decide to become smokers. We merely experiment with the first few attempts and, because they taste awful, we are convinced that we can stop whenever we want to. In the main we smoke those first few cigarettes only when we want to, and that is usually in the company of other smokers on social occasions.

Before we realise it, we are not only buying them regularly, not only smoking when we want to, now we are smoking continuously.

It usually takes us a long time to realise that we are hooked because we suffer the illusion that smokers smoke because they enjoy a cigarette, not because they have to have a cigarette, and, whilst we are not enjoying them (which we never do), we suffer the illusion that we can stop whenever we want to.

Usually it is not until we actually try to stop that we realise a problem exists. The first attempts to stop are more often than not in the early days and are usually triggered off by shortage of money (boy meets girl and they are saving to set-up home and do not want to waste money on cigarettes) or health (the teenager is still active in sport and finds he is short of breath). Whatever the reason the smoker always waits for a stress situation whether it be health, or money. As soon as he stops, the little monster needs feeding. The smoker then wants a cigarette and because he cannot have one this makes him more distressed. The thing he usually takes to relieve stress is now not available and so he suffers a triple blow. The probable result after a period of torture is either the compromise "I'll cut down" or "I've picked the wrong time" or "I'll wait until the stress has gone from my life." However once the stress has gone, he has no need to stop and doesn't decide to do so again until the next stressfull time. Of course the time is never right because life for most people doesn't become less stressfull it becomes more so. We leave the protection of our parents and enter the world of setting-up home, taking-on mortgages, having children, and more responsible jobs etc. Of course the smoker's life can never become less stressful because it is the cigarette that actually causes stress. As the smoker's rate of nicotine intake rises, the more distressed he becomes and the greater the illusion of his dependency becomes.

After the initial failures the smoker usually relies on the possibility that one day he will wake up and just not want to smoke anymore. This hope is usually kindled by the stories that he has heard about other ex-smokers e.g. "I had a bout of 'flu and afterwards I didn't want to smoke anymore".

Don't kid yourself, I have probed all of these rumours and they are never quite as simple as they appear. Usually the smoker has already been preparing himself to stop and merely used the 'flu as a springboard. I spent 25 years waiting to wake up one morning and never wanting to smoke again. Whenever I had a bad chest I would look forward to it's ending because it was interfering with my smoking.

More often, with these cases of people that stop "JUST LIKE THAT", they have suffered a shock. Perhaps a close relative has died from a cigarette-related disease or they have had a scare themselves. It is so much easier to say "I just decided to stop one day, that's the sort of chap I am". Stop kidding yourself! It won't happen unless you make it happen.

Let's just consider in greater detail why the Willpower Method is so difficult. For most of our lives it is the head-in-the-sand "I'll stop tomorrow".

At odd times something will trigger-off an attempt to stop. It may be health, money, social stigma or that we have been going through a particularly heavy bout of choking ourselves and we realise that we don't actually enjoy it.

Whatever the reason, we take our head out of the sand and start weighing up the pros and cons of smoking. We then find what we have known all our lives i.e. on a rational assessment the answer is a dozen times over – STOP SMOKING.

If you were to sit down and give all the advantages from stopping points out of ten and do a similar exercise with the advantages of smoking, the total point count for stopping will far outweigh the disadvantages.

However, although the smoker knows that he will be better off as a non-smoker, he does believe that he is making a sacrifice. Although it is an illusion, it is a powerful illusion. The smoker doesn't know why but he does believe that during the good times and the bad times of life, the cigarette does appear to help.

Before he starts the attempt he has the brainwashing from our society, reinforced by the brainwashing of his own addiction. To these must be added the even more powerful brainwashing of "How difficult it is to give up".

He has heard of stories of smokers who have stopped for many months and are still desperately craving a cigarette. There are all the disgruntled stoppers i.e. people who stop and then spend the rest of their lives bemoaning the fact that they'd love a cigarette. He has heard of cases where smokers, who have stopped for many years apparently leading happy lives, have one cigarette and are suddenly hooked again and can't stop. Probably, he also knows several smokers in the advanced stages of the disease who are visibly destroying themselves and are clearly not enjoying the cigarette – yet they continue to smoke. Added to all this he probably has already suffered one or more of these experiences himself.

So, instead of starting with the feeling "Great! have you heard the news? I haven't got to smoke anymore" he starts with a feeling of doom and gloom, as if he is trying to climb Everest, and he firmly believes that once the little monster has got his hooks into you – you are hooked for life. Many smokers even start the attempt by apologising to their friends and relatives with something like "Look I am trying to give-up smoking, I will probably be irritable during the next few weeks, try to bear with me" etc. Most attempts are doomed before they start.

Let's assume that the smoker survives a few days without a cigarette. The congestion is rapidly disappearing from his lungs. He hasn't bought cigarettes and consequently has more money in his pocket. So the reasons that he decided to stop in the first place are rapidly disappearing from his thoughts. It is like seeing a bad road accident when you are driving, it slows you down for a while but the next time you are late for an appointment you have forgotten all about it and it's foot on the throttle.

On the other side of the tug of war that little monster inside your stomach hasn't had his fix. There is no physical pain; if you had the same feeling because of a cold you wouldn't even stop work or get depressed, you would laugh it off. All the smoker knows is that he wants a cigarette. Quite why it is so important to him he doesn't know – just that he needs a cigarette. The little monster in the stomach then starts off the big monster in the mind and now the person that a few hours or days earlier was listing all the reasons to stop, is desperately searching for any valid excuse to start again. Now he is saying things like:

1   Life is too short, the bomb could go off, I could step under a bus tomorrow or I have left it too late or they tell you everything gives you cancer these days"   *or*
2   "I have picked the wrong time. I should have waited until after Christmas, after my holidays, after this stressful event in my life"   *or*
3   The one that kept me smoking for 25 years "I cannot concentrate, I am getting irritable and bad tempered. I cannot do my job properly. My family and friends won't love me. Lets face it for everybodies' sake I have got to start smoking again. I am a confirmed smoker and there is no way I will ever be happy again without a cigarette".

At this stage the smoker usually gives in. He lights a cigarette and the schizophrenia is increased. On the one hand there is the tremendous relief of ending the craving, when the little monster finally gets his fix and on the other hand, if he survived a long time the cigarette tastes awful and the smoker cannot understand why he is smoking it. This is why the smoker thinks he lacks willpower. In fact it is not lack of willpower all he has done is changed his mind and in fact he had made a perfectly rational decision in the light of the latest information – What's the point of being healthy if you are miserable? What is the point of being rich if you are miserable? Absolutely none. Far better to have a shorter enjoyable life than a lengthy miserable life.

Fortunately it is not true, just the reverse. Life as a non-smoker is infinitely more enjoyable but it was this criteria that kept me smoking for 25 years and I must confess, if that were the true situation, I would still be smoking (correction – I wouldn't be here).

The misery that the smoker is suffering is actually nothing to do with withdrawal pangs. True they trigger them off, but the actual agony is in the mind and it is caused by the doubt and uncertainty. Because the smoker starts by feeling he is making a sacrifice, he begins to feel deprived – this is a form of stress. One of the times when his brain triggers "Have a cigarette" is a time of stress. Therefore as soon as he stops he wants a cigarette. But now he can't have one because he has stopped smoking. This makes him more depressed which sets the trigger off again.

Another thing that makes it so difficult is the waiting for something to happen. If your object is to pass a driving test, as soon as you have passed the test, it is certain you have achieved your object. Under the Willpower Method you say:

"If I can go long enough without a cigarette the urge to smoke will eventually go".

How do you know when you have achieved it? The answer is, you never do, because you are waiting for something to happen and nothing else is going to happen. You actually stopped when you smoked that last cigarette and what you are really doing now is waiting to see how long before you give in.

As I said above the actual agony that the smoker undergoes is in fact mental, caused by the uncertainty. Although there is no physical pain it still has a powerful effect. The smoker is miserable and feeling insecure. Far from forgetting about smoking his mind becomes obsessed with it.

There can be days or even weeks of Black Depression. His mind is obsessed with doubts and fears.

"How long will the craving last?"

"Will I ever be happy again?"

"Will I ever want to get up in the morning?"

"Will I ever enjoy a meal again?"

"How will I ever cope with stress in future?"

"Will I ever enjoy a social function again?"

The smoker is waiting for things to improve but of course while he is still moping about them, the cigarette isn't becoming less precious it becomes more precious.

In fact something does happen but the smoker isn't conscious of it. If he can survive three weeks without inhaling any nicotine at all, the physical craving for nicotine disappears. However, as stated before the actual withdrawal pangs from nicotine are so mild that the smoker isn't aware of them. But after about three weeks many smokers sense that they have "kicked it" they then light a cigarette to prove it and it does just that. It tastes awful and fills the ex-smoker with a warm secure glow. But he has now put fresh nicotine into the body and as soon as he extinguishes that cigarette the nicotine starts to leave the body and there is now a little voice at the back of his mind saying "You want another one". In fact he had kicked it but now he has hooked himself again.

Smokers that succeed under the Willpower Method tend to find it long and difficult. Because the main problem is the brainwashing and long after the physical addiction has died the smoker is still moping about cigarettes. Eventually, if he can survive long enough, it begins to dawn on him that he is not going to give in. He stops moping and accepts that life goes on and it is in fact enjoyable without the cigarette.

Many smokers are succeeding with this method, but it is difficult and arduous and there are many more failures than successes. Even those that do succeed go through the rest of their lives in a vulnerable state. They are left with a certain degree of the brainwashing and believe that during good and bad times the cigarette can give you a boost. (Most non-smokers also suffer the illusion. They are subjected to the brainwashing also but either find they cannot learn to "enjoy" them or don't want the bad side, thank you very much. This explains why many smokers that have stopped for long periods start smoking again. It is usually brought about by a serious trauma in their lives or more often its a social occasion a Wedding, Xmas etc. Many ex-smokers will have the occasional cigar or cigarette either as "a special treat" or to convince themselves how awful they are. It does exactly that but as soon as they put it out the nicotine starts to leave and a little voice at the back of their mind is saying:

"You want another one".

If they light another one it still tastes awful and they say:

"Marvellous! Whilst I am not enjoying them I won't get hooked. After Xmas or after the holiday or trauma I will stop."

Too late they are already hooked. The same trap that they fell into in the first place has claimed its victim again.

As I keep saying, "Enjoyment" doesn't come into it. It never did! If we smoked because we enjoy them, nobody would ever smoke more than one cigarette. We only assume we enjoy them because we cannot believe we would be so stupid as to smoke if we didn't enjoy them. We smoke to feed that little monster ... and once you have purged the "Little Monster" from your body and the "Big Monster" from your brain, you will have neither need nor desire to smoke!

23

Beware of Cutting-Down

Many smokers resort to "cutting-down" either as a stepping stone towards stopping or as an attempt to control the little monster and many doctors and advisers of giving-up smoking recommend first cutting-down as an aid.

Obviously the less you smoke the better off you are, but as a stepping stone to stopping, cutting-down is fatal. In fact it is our attempts to cut-down that keep us trapped all our lives.

Usually cutting-down follows failed attempts to stop. After a few hours or days of abstinence the smoker says to himself something like:

"I cannot face the thought of being without a cigarette so from now on I will just smoke the special ones or I will cut down to ten a day. If I can get in the habit of smoking ten a day I can either hold it there or cut down further.

Certain terrible things now happen viz:

1   He has the worst of all worlds. He is still addicted to nicotine and not only keeping the monster alive in his body but also in his mind.
2   He is now wishing his life away just waiting for the next cigarette.
3   Prior to cutting down, whenever he wanted a cigarette he lit one up and at least partially relieved his withdrawal pangs. Now, in addition to the normal stress and strains of life, he is actually causing himself to suffer the withdrawal pangs from nicotine most of his life. So he is now actually causing himself to be miserable and bad tempered.
4   Whilst he was indulging himself, not only didn't he enjoy most of the cigarettes, he didn't realise he was smoking them. It was automatic. The only cigarettes that he suffered the delusion of enjoying were after a period of abstinence e.g. the first in the morning, the one after a meal etc.

Now that he waits an extra hour for each cigarette, he enjoys every cigarette. The longer he waits the more enjoyable each cigarette appears to become, because the enjoyment in a cigarette isn't the cigarette itself, it's the ending of the agitation caused by the craving. The longer you suffer, the more enjoyable each cigarette becomes.

The main difficulty of giving up smoking is not the chemical addiction, that's easy. Smokers will go all night without a cigarette, it doesn't even wake them up. Many smoker will actually leave the bedroom before they light-up. Many will actually have breakfast. Some will even wait until they arrive at work.

They will go ten hours without a cigarette and it doesn't bother them. If they went ten hours during the day without one they would be tearing their hair out.

Many smokers will buy a new car and abstain from smoking in it. Smokers will visit supermarkets, theatres, doctors, hospitals, dentists etc. without undue inconvenience. Many smokers will abstain in the company of non-smokers. Even on the tube trains there have been no riots, smokers are almost pleased for some one to say you cannot smoke. In fact smokers get a secret pleasure going long periods without a cigarette, it gives them the hope that maybe one day they will never want another one.

The real problem of giving up smoking is the brainwashing. The illusion that the cigarette is some sort of prop or reward that life will never be quite the same without it. Far from turning you off of smoking, all cutting-down does is to leave you feeling insecure and miserable and convinces you that the most precious thing on this earth is the next cigarette and that there is no way that you will ever be happy again without one.

There is nothing more pathetic than the smoker who is trying to cut down. He suffers the delusion that, the less he smokes, the less he will want to smoke. In fact it is just the reverse. The less he smokes, the longer he suffers the withdrawal pangs, the more he enjoys the cigarette, the more distasteful they become. But that won't stop you smoking. Taste never ever came into it. If smokers, smoked because they enjoyed the taste, nobody would ever smoke more than one cigarette. You find that difficult to believe? O.K., let us talk it out. Which is the worst tasting cigarette? That's right, the first in the morning, the one that in winter sets us coughing, and spluttering. Which is one of the most precious cigarettes for most smokers? That's right the first cigarette in the morning! Now do you really believe you are smoking it to enjoy the taste and smell, or do you think a more rational explanation is that you are relieving nine hours withdrawal pangs?

Cutting-down not only doesn't work, it is the worst form of torture. It doesn't work because initially the smoker hopes that by getting into the habit of smoking less and less he will reduce his desire to smoke a ciga-rette. It is not a habit it is "an addiction" and the nature of any addic-tion is to want more and more not less and less. Therefore in order to cut-down, the smoker has to exercise willpower and discipline for the rest of his life.

The main problem of stopping smoking is not the chemical addiction to nicotine, that's easy to cope with. It is the mistaken belief that the cigarette gives you some pleasure. This mistaken belief is brought about initially by the brainwashing we receive before we start smoking which is then reinforced by the actual addiction. All cutting-down does is to further reinforce the fallacy to the extent that smoking dominates the smoker's life completely and convinces him that the most precious thing on this earth is the next cigarette.

As I have already said, cutting-down never works anyway because you have to exercise willpower and discipline for the rest of your life. If you had not enough willpower to stop then you certainly have not got enough to cut-down. Stopping is the far easier and less painful of the two evils.

I have heard of literally thousands of cases where cutting-down fails. Of the handful that I have known where it worked, this was after a rela-tively short period of cutting-down followed by the "Cold Turkey" in which case the smoker really stopped in spite of cutting-down, not because of it. All it did was to prolong the agony. A failed attempt to cut-down leaves the smoker a nervous wreck even more convinced that he is hooked for life. This is usually good enough to keep him puffing away for another five years before the next attempt.

However cutting down does help to illustrate the whole futility of the smoking habit because it does clearly illustrate that a cigarette is only enjoyable after a period of abstinence i.e. you have to bang your head against a brick wall (i.e. suffer withdrawal pangs) to make it nice when you stop.

So the choice is:

1 Cutting-down for life. Self-imposed torture and you will not be able to do it anyway,
2 Having to increasingly choke yourself for life. What is the point? *or*
3 Be nice to yourself and give it up.

The other important aspect that cutting down demonstrates is that there is no such thing as the odd cigarette, the occasional cigarette. It is a chain reaction which will last the rest of your life, unless you make a positive effort to break it.

REMEMBER CUTTING DOWN WILL DRAG YOU DOWN

24

Just One Cigarette

"Just one cigarette" is another myth you must get out of your mind.

It is one cigarette that gets us started in the first place.

It is just one cigarette to tide us over a difficult patch or a cigarette on a special occasion that defeats most of our attempts to stop.

It is just one cigarette that, when smokers have succeeded in breaking the addiction sends them back into the trap. Sometimes it is just to confirm that they do not need them anymore and that one cigarette does just that. It tastes horrible and convinces the smoker he will never become hooked again, but he already has.

It is the thought of that one special cigarette which often prevents smokers from stopping. The first one in the morning or the one after a meal.

Get it firmly in your mind there is no such thing as one cigarette. It is a chain reaction, which will last the rest of your life, unless you break it.

It is the myth about the odd, special cigarette that keeps smokers moping about it when they stop. Get into the habit of never seeing the odd cigarette or packet – it is a fantasy. Whenever you think about smoking, see the whole filthy lifetime of spending a small fortune just for the privilege of destroying yourself mentally and physically, a lifetime of slavery, a lifetime of bad breath etc. etc.

It is a pity that there isn't something like a cigarette that during good and bad times we can use as an occasional boost or pleasure. But get it clearly into your mind the cigarette isn't "it". You are stuck with either a lifetime of misery or none at all. You wouldn't dream of taking cyanide because you liked the taste of almonds so stop punishing yourself with the thought of the occasional cigarette or cigar.

Another strange aspect about smoking is ask a smoker "If you had the opportunity to go back to the time before you became hooked, would you have become a smoker?" The answer is inevitably "You have got to be joking", and yet every smoker has that choice everyday of his life. Why doesn't he opt for it? The answer is fear. The fear that he cannot stop or that life won't be the same without it.

Stop kidding yourself, you can do it, anybody can, its ridiculously easy.

In order to make it easy to stop smoking there are certain fundamentals to get clearly in your mind. We have already dealt with three of them up to now viz.

1 There is nothing to give up. Only marvellous positive gains to achieve.
2 Never see the odd cigarette, it doesn't exist, only the lifetime of filth and disease.
3 There is nothing different about you, any smoker can find it easy to stop.

25

Casual Smokers, Teenagers, Non-smokers

Heavy smokers tend to envy the casual smoker. Don't, in a peculiar way the casual smoker is more hooked and miserable than the heavy smoker. It is true that he is less vulnerable to the fearful physical risks to his health and that he would not be spending as much money as you. However, in other ways he is far worse off.

Remember no smoker actually enjoys cigarettes, all they enjoy is relieving withdrawal pangs. The natural tendency of the drug is to relieve withdrawal pangs, not to suffer them. Therefore the natural tendency is to chain smoke.

There are three main factors that prevent smokers from chain smoking:

1 MONEY: Most cannot afford to.
2 HEALTH: In order to relieve our withdrawal pangs we have to intake a poisonous product. Our capacity to cope with that poison varies with each individual and at different times and situations in his or her life. This acts as an automatic restraint.
3 DISCIPLINE: Either imposed by society or the smoker's job or friends and relatives, or, imposed by the smoker himself as a result of the natural tug of war that goes on in every smokers mind.

It may be of advantage at this stage to detail a few definitions.

A. NON-SMOKER: Is someone who has never fallen for the trap. Do not be complacent. They are only non-smokers by the grace of God. All smokers were convinced that they would never become hooked and another pathetic aspect of the subject is how hard some non-smokers keep trying that occasional cigarette.
B. CASUAL SMOKERS: There are two basic classifications of casual smokers:

1 The smoker who has fallen for the trap, but doesn't realise it. Do not envy these smokers. They are merely on the first rung of the ladder and in all probability will soon be heavy smokers. Remember you started off as a casual smoker.

2 The smoker that was previously a heavy smoker and thinks he cannot stop. These are the most pathetic of all. They fall into various categories each of which needs separate comment.

THE FIVE-A-DAY SMOKER

If they enjoy a cigarette why do they only smoke five-a-day? If they can take it or leave it, why do they bother to smoke at all? Remember the habit is really banging your head against the brick wall to make it relaxing when you stop. The five-a-day smoker is relieving his withdrawal pangs for less than one hour each day. The rest of the day, although he doesn't realise it, he is banging his head against the wall and does so for most of his life. He is only smoking five-a-day because either he cannot afford to smoke more or he is worried about the health risk. It is easy to convince the heavy smoker that he doesn't enjoy it, but you try convincing a casual smoker. Anybody who has gone through an attempt to cut down will know it is the worst torture of all and almost guaranteed to keep you hooked the rest of your life.

THE MORNING OR EVENING ONLY SMOKER

He punishes himself by suffering withdrawal pangs for half the day in order to relieve them the other half. Again ask him why, if he enjoys a cigarette, that he doesn't smoke the whole day, or, if he doesn't enjoy a cigarette, why he bothers at all.

THE SIX MONTHS ON SIX MONTHS OFF SMOKER

(Or "I can stop whenever I want to, I have done it thousands of times".) If they enjoy smoking, why do they stop for six months? If they do not enjoy it, why do they start again? The truth is they are still hooked. Although they get rid of the physical addiction they are left with the main problem – the brainwashing. The truth is really that they hope that each time they will stop for good and soon fall for the trap again.

THE "I ONLY SMOKE ON SPECIAL OCCASIONS" SMOKER

Yes we all do to start with, but isn't it amazing how the number of occasions seem to rapidly increase and that before we know it we seem to be smoking on all occasions?

THE "I HAVE STOPPED BUT I HAVE AN OCCASIONAL CIGAR/CIGARETTE"

In a way these are the most pathetic of all. They either go through their lives believing they are being deprived. More often, the occasional cigar becomes two. They remain on the slippery slope and it goes only one way – DOWNWARDS. Sooner or later they are back to being heavy smokers. They have fallen for the same trap that they fell into in the first place.

Do not envy casual smokers for they are the most pathetic of all. I recently had a case of a five-a-day man. He started the telephone conversation in a croaky "Mr. Carr, I just want to stop smoking before I die". This is how that man described his life.

"I am 61 years old. I have got cancer of the throat through smoking. Now I can only physically cope with five 'roll ups' a day.

"I used to sleep soundly through the night, now I wake up every hour of the night and all I can think about is cigarettes. Even when I am sleeping, I dream about smoking.

"I cannot smoke my first cigarette until 10 o'clock. I get up at 5 o'clock and make endless cups of tea. My wife gets up at about 8 o'clock and because I am so bad tempered, she will not have me in the house. I go down to the greenhouse and try to potter about, but my mind is obsessed with smoking. At 9 o'clock I begin to roll my first cigarette and I do so until it is perfect. It is not that I need it to be perfect, but it gives me something to do. I then wait for 10 o'clock. When it arrives my hands are shaking uncontrollably. I do not light the cigarette then. If I do, I have to wait three hours for the next one. Eventually I light the cigarette, take one puff and extinguish it immediately. By continuing this process I can make the cigarette last one hour. I smoke it down to about a quarter of an inch and then wait for the next one."

In addition to his other troubles, this poor man had burns all over his lips caused by smoking the cigarette too low. You probably have visions of a pathetic imbecile. Not so. This man was over 6 feet tall and an ex-sergeant in the marines. He was a former athelete and didn't want to become a smoker. However in the last war, society believed that cigarettes gave courage and servicemen were issued free rations of them. This man was virtually ordered to become a smoker. He has spent the rest of his life paying through the nose, subsidising other peoples taxes and it has ruined him physically and mentally. If he were an animal our society would have put him out of his misery and yet still we allow mentally and physically healthy young teenagers to become hooked!

You may think the above case is exaggerated, it is extreme, but not unique. There are literally thousands of similar stories. That man poured his heart out to me but you can be sure that many of his friends and acquaintances envied him for being a five-a-day man. If you think this couldn't happen to you, STOP KIDDING YOURSELF.

IT IS ALREADY HAPPENING!!!

In any event smokers are notorious liars, even to themselves, they have to be. Most casual smokers smoke far more cigarettes and on far more occasions than they will admit to. I have had many conversations with the so called five-a-day smoker during which they have smoked more than five cigarettes in my presence. Observe casual smokers at social events such as weddings and parties. They will be chain smoking like the best of them.

In any event, get it into your head that you do not need to envy casual smokers. You do not need to smoke, it is an illusion. Not only is life just as sweet without them it is infinitely more so!!!

Teenagers are generally more difficult to cure, not because they find it more difficult to stop, but because either they do not believe they are hooked or because they are only at the primary stage of the disease and suffer the delusion that they will automatically have stopped before the secondary stage.

I would like particularly to warn parents of children that loathe smoking not to have a false sense of security. All children loathe the smell and taste of tobacco until they become hooked. You did too at one time. Also do not be fooled by the Government scare campaigns. The trap is the same as it always was. Children know that cigarettes kill you but they also know that one cigarette will not do it. At some stage they may be influenced by a girlfriend or boyfriend, schoolfriend or work colleague. All they need is to try one they will taste horrible and convince them they would never become hooked. Warn your children of the full facts!!!

26

The Secret Smoker

The secret smoker should be grouped with casual smokers but the effects of secret smoking are so insidious that it merits a separate chapter. It can lead to the breakdown of personal relationships. In my case it nearly caused a divorce.

I was three weeks into one of my failed attempts to stop. The attempt had been triggered off by my wife being worried about my constant wheezing and coughing. I had told her I was not worried about my health. She said I know you are not, but how would you feel if you had to watch someone you love systematically destroying themselves. It was an argument that I found irresistable, hence the attempt to stop. The attempt ended after 3 weeks after a heated argument with an old friend. It did not register until years afterwards that my devious mind had deliberately triggered-off the argument. I felt justly aggrieved at the time but I do not believe that it was just coincidence as I had never argued with this particular friend before or since. It was clearly the little monster at work. Anyway I had my excuse. I desperately needed a cigarette and started smoking again.

I could not bear the disappointment this would cause my wife so I did not tell her. I just smoked when alone. Then gradually I would smoke in the company of friends until it got to the point where everybody knew I was smoking except my wife. I remember being quite pleased at the time. I thought, "well at least it is cutting my consumption down". Eventually she accused me of continuing to smoke. I had not realised it but she described the times I had caused an argument and stormed out of the house. Other times, when I had taken two hours to purchase some menial item and on occasions where I would normally have invited her to accompany me, I had made feeble excuses to go alone.

As the anti-social split between smokers and non-smokers widens there are literally thousands of cases where the company of friends or relatives is shortened or avoided because of this awful little weed. The worst thing about secret smoking is that it increases the fallacy in the smoker's mind that he is being deprived. At the same time, it causes a

70

major loss of self respect so that an otherwise honest person may deceive his family and friends.

If you think about it, it has probably happened or is still happening to you in some form. Another evil or this filthy weed.

27

A Social Habit?

The main reason that there are over ten million ex-smokers in Britain since the 1960s is the social revolution that is taking place.

Yes, I know, health followed by money are the main reasons we should want to stop but then they always have been. We do not actually need the cancer scare etc. to tell us that cigarettes shatter our lives. These bodies of ours are the most sophisticated objects on the planet and any smoker knows instantly from the first puff that cigarettes are poisonous.

The only reason we ever get involved with smoking is the social pressures of our friends. The only valid "plus" smoking ever had was that it was at one time considered a perfectly acceptable social habit.

Today it is generally considered, even by smokers themselves, to be an anti-social habit.

In the old days the strong man smoked. If you didn't smoke you were considered to be a cissy and we all worked very hard to become hooked. In every Public House, or club bar, the majority of men would proudly be inhaling and exhaling tobacco smoke. There would be the permanent fall-out cloud and all ceilings which were not regularly decorated soon became yellow or brown.

Today the position is completely reversed. Today's strong man doesn't need to smoke, today's strong man is not dependent on a drug.

With the social revolution all smokers nowadays are giving serious thoughts about stopping and today's smokers are considered to be generally weak people.

28

Timing

Apart from the obvious, that as it is doing you no good, now is the right time to stop, I believe timing is important. Our society treats smoking flippantly as a slightly distasteful habit that can injure your health. It is not, it is drug addiction, a disease and the No. 1 killer in Western society. The worst thing that happens in most smokers' lives is getting hooked on that awful weed. If they stay hooked, horrendous things happen. Timing is important to give yourself the right to a proper cure.

First of all decide the times or occasions when smoking appears to be important to you. If you are a businesman and smoke for the illusion of relief of stress, pick a relatively slack period, a good idea is to devote your annual holiday. If you mainly smoke during boring or relaxing periods, do the opposite. In any event take the matter seriously and make the attempt the most important thing in your life. Look ahead for a period of about three weeks and try to anticipate any event which might lead to failure. Occasions like a wedding or Christmas, need not deter you, providing you anticipate them in advance and do not feel you will be deprived. Do not attempt to cut-down in the meantime as this will only create the illusion that the cigarette is enjoyable. In fact it helps to force as many of the filthy things down your throat as possible. While you are smoking that last cigarette, be conscious of the bad smell and taste and think how marvellous it will be when you allow yourself to stop doing it.

WHATEVER YOU DO, DON'T FALL INTO THE TRAP OF JUST SAYING "NOT NOW, LATER" AND PUTTING IT OUT OF YOUR MIND. WORK OUT YOUR TIMETABLE NOW AND LOOK FORWARD TO IT. Remember you aren't giving anything up. On the contrary you are about to receive marvellous positive gains.

29

Will I Miss the Cigarette?

No! Once that little nicotine monster is dead and your body stops craving nicotine, any remaining brainwashing will vanish and you will find that you will be both physically and mentally better equipped to cope not only with stresses and strains of life, but to enjoy the good times to the full.

There is only one danger and that is the influence of people still smoking. "The other man's grass is always greener" is commonplace in many aspects of our lives and is easily understandable. Why is it in the case of smoking, where the disadvantages are so enormous as compared with even the "illusionary" advantages, that ex-smokers tend to envy the smoker?

With all the brainwashing of our childhood it is quite understandable that we fall into the trap. Why is it that once we realise what a mug's game it is and when many of us manage to kick the habit, that we walk straight back into the same trap? It is the influence of smokers.

It usually happens on social occasions, particularly after a meal. The smoker lights up and the ex-smoker has a pang. This is indeed a curious anomaly, particularly if you consider this piece of market research: Not only is every non-smoker in the world happy to be a non-smoker, but every smoker in the world, even with his warped, addicted, brainwashed mind suffering the delusion that he enjoys it or it relaxes him, wishes he had never become hooked in the first place. So why do some ex-smokers envy the smoker on these occasions? There are two reasons viz.

1   "Just one cigarette", remember it doesn't exist. Stop seeing that isolated occasion and start looking at it from the point of view of the smoker. You may be envying him but he doesn't envy himself, he envies you. Start observing other smokers. They can be the most powerful boost of all to help you off it. Notice on that social occasion how quickly the cigarette burns, how quickly the smoker

74

has to light-up another. Notice particularly that not only is he not aware that he is smoking the cigarette but even the lighting-up appears to be automatic. Remember he is not enjoying it, it's just that he cannot enjoy himself without it. Particularly remember when he leaves your company he is going to have to go on smoking. The next morning, when he wakes up with a chest like a cesspit, he is going to have to carry on choking himself. The next Budget day, the next time he has a pain in the chest, the next National Non-Smoking Day, the next time he inadvertently sees the Government Health Warning, the next time there is a cancer scare, the next time he is in church, on a tube train, visiting a hospital, library, dentist, doctor, supermarket etc. The next time he is in the company of a non-smoker he has to continue this lifetime chain of paying through the nose just for the privilege of destroying himself physically and mentally, a lifetime of filth, bad breath, stained teeth; a lifetime of slavery, a lifetime of destroying himself, a lifetime of black shadows at the back of his mind. All of this is to achieve what purpose? The illusion of trying to get back to the state he was in before he became hooked in the first place.

2   The second reason that some smokers have pangs on these occasions is the negative aspect. Because the smoker is doing something i.e. smoking the cigarette, and the non-smoker is not, he tends to feel deprived. Get it clearly in your mind before you start, it is not the non-smoker that is being deprived, it is the poor smoker being deprived of:

HEALTH
ENERGY
MONEY
CONFIDENCE
PEACE OF MIND
COURAGE
TRANQUILLITY
FREEDOM
SELF RESPECT.

Get out of the habit of envying smokers and start seeing them as the miserable, pathetic creatures they really are. I know I was the world's worst. That is why you are reading the book and the ones that cannot face up to it, that have to go on kidding themselves, are the most pathetic of all.

You wouldn't envy a heroin addict, so don't envy the poor nicotine addicts.

HAVE PITY ON THEM!

30

Will I Put on Weight?

This is another myth about smoking and is caused mainly by smokers who, when attempting to stop under the "Willpower" Method, substitute sweets etc., to help relieve withdrawal pangs.

In fact the reverse is the case. The withdrawal pangs of nicotine are very similar to hunger pangs and the two are easily confused. However, whereas the pangs of hunger can be satisfied by food, the withdrawal pangs from nicotine are never completely satisfied.

Like any drug after a while, the body becomes immune and the drug ceases to completely relieve the withdrawal pangs. As soon as we extinguish the cigarette, the nicotine rapidly leaves our body so that the nicotine addict has a permanent hunger. The natural inclination is eventually to chain smoke. However, most smokers are prevented from doing this because of one or both of two reasons.

1   Money – They cannot afford to increase their intake   *or*
2   Health – In order to relieve the withdrawal pangs we have to intake a poison. This acts as an automatic check on the number of cigarettes we can smoke.

The poor smoker is therefore left with a permanent hunger which he can never satisfy. This is why many smokers turn to over-eating, heavy drinking or even harder drugs in order to satisfy the void. (MOST ALCOHOLICS ARE HEAVY SMOKERS. I WONDER IF IT IS REALLY A SMOKING PROBLEM?)

The normal tendency with the smoker is to start by substituting nicotine for food. During my own nightmare years I got to the stage where I cut out breakfast and lunch completely. I would chain smoke during the day. In the later years I would actually look forward to the evenings only for the reason that I could stop smoking. However, I would be picking at food all evening. I thought it was hunger but it was really the withdrawal pangs from nicotine. In other words, during the day I would substitute nicotine for food and during the evenings I would substitute food for nicotine.

In those days I was two stone heavier than I am now and there was nothing I could do about it.

Once that little monster leaves your body, that awful feeling of insecurity ends. Your confidence returns together with a marvellous feeling of self-respect. You obtain the assurance to take control of your life, not only in your eating habits but also in all other ways. This is one of the many great advantages of being free from the weed.

As I have said the "weight myth" is due to using substitutes during the withdrawal period. In fact they do not make it easier to stop, they make it harder. This is explained in greater detail in a later chapter dealing with substitutes.

31

Avoid False Incentives

Many smokers, whilst trying to stop under the Willpower Method, try to increase the incentive to stop by building up false incentives.

There are many examples of this. A typical one is "My family and I can have a marvellous holiday on the money I will save". This appears to be a logical and sensible approach, but in fact it is false because any self-respecting smoker would rather smoke 52 weeks in the year and not have a holiday. In any case there is a doubt in the smoker's mind because not only will he have to abstain for 50 weeks, but will he even enjoy that holiday without a cigarette? All this does is to increase the sacrifice that the smoker feels he is making, which makes the cigarette even more precious in his mind. Instead, concentrate on the other side: "What am I getting out of it, why do I need to smoke?" Another example "I'll be able to afford a better car". That's true and the incentive might make you abstain until you get that car but once the novelty has gone, you will feel deprived and sooner or later you will fall for the trap again.

Another typical example is to have an office or family pact. These do have the advantage of eliminating temptation for certain periods of the day. However, they generally fail due to the following reasons:

1   The incentive is false. Why should you want to stop smoking just because other people are doing so. All this does is to create an additional pressure which increases the element of sacrifice. It is fine if all smokers genuinely want to stop at that particular time. However, you cannot force smokers to stop and although all smokers secretly want to, until they are ready to do so the pact just creates additional pressure which increases their desire to smoke. This turns them into secret smokers which further increases the feeling of dependency.

2   The "Rotten Apple" theory, or dependency on each other. Under the Willpower Method of stopping the smoker is undergoing a period of penance waiting for the urge to smoke to go. If he "gives in" there is a sense of failure. Under the Willpower Method sooner or later one of the participants is bound to give in, the

other participants now have the excuse they have been waiting for. It's not their fault, they would have held out, it is just Fred that let us down. The truth is that most of them have already been cheating.

3 "Sharing the credit" is the reverse of the "Rotten Apple" theory. Here the loss of face due to failure is not so bad when shared. There is a marvellous sense of achievement in stopping smoking and when you are doing it alone the emphasis of the limelight you receive from your friends, relatives and colleagues can be a tremendous boost to help you over the first few days. When everybody is doing it at the same time, the credit has to be shared and the boost is consequently reduced.

Another classic example of false incentives is the bribe e.g. the parent offering the teenager a sum of money to abstain or the bet "I will bet you £100 if I fail". There was a recent example in a T.V. programme. A policeman trying to give up smoking put a £20 note in his cigarette packet. He had a pact with himself. He could smoke again but he had to set light first to the £20 note. This stopped him for a few days but eventually he burnt the note.

Stop kidding yourself. If the £25,000 that the average smoker spends in his life won't stop him, or the one-in-four risk of horrendous diseases or the lifetime of bad breath, mental and physical torture, slavery, being despised by most of the population and despising yourself, a few phoney incentives will not make the slightest bit of difference, they will only make the sacrifice appear worse. Keep looking at the other side of the tug of war:

What is it doing for me?   ABSOLUTELY NOTHING!
Why do I need to do it?   YOU DON'T!
YOU ARE ONLY PUNISHING YOURSELF!

32

The Easy Way to Stop

This chapter contains instructions on the easy way to stop smoking. Providing you follow the instructions you will find it ranging from relatively easy to enjoyable! But remember the definition of a brunette is "A girl who didn't read the instructions on the bottle".

It is ridiculously easy to stop smoking, all you have to do is two things.

1   Make the decision that you are never going to smoke again.
2   Don't mope about it, rejoice about it.

You are probably asking "Why the need for the rest of the book?" "Why couldn't you have just said that in the first place?" The answer is that you would at some time have moped about it and consequently sooner or later you would have changed your decision. "You have probably already done it many times before."

As I have already said the whole business of smoking is a subtle sinister trap. The main problem of stopping isn't the chemical addiction but the brainwashing and it was necessary to first explode the myths and delusions. Understand your enemy, know his tactics and you will easily defeat him.

I've spent most of my life trying to stop smoking and suffered weeks of black depression. When I finally stopped I went from a hundred a day to ZERO without one bad moment. It was enjoyable even during the withdrawal period and I have never had the slightest pang since. On the contrary it is the most wonderful thing that has happened in my life.

I couldn't understand why it had been so easy and it took me a long time to find out the reason. It was this. I knew for certain that I was never going to smoke again. On previous attempts, no matter how determined I was, I was basically trying to stop smoking, hoping that if I could survive long enough without one, the urge would eventually go. Of course it didn't go because I was waiting for something to happen and the more I moped about it, the more I wanted a cigarette so the urge never went. My final attempt was different. Like all smokers nowadays, I had been giving the problem serious thought. Up to then, whenever I failed I had consoled myself with the thought that it would be easier next time. It had never occurred to me that I would have to go on smoking the rest of my life. This latter thought filled me with horror and started me thinking very deeply into the subject.

Instead of lighting-up each cigarette subconsciously, I started to analyse my feelings as I was smoking them. This confirmed what I already knew. Not only wasn't I enjoying them but they were filthy and disgusting.

I started looking at non-smokers. Up till then I had always visualised non-smokers as wishy-washy, unsociable, finicky type people. However, when I examined them they appeared, if anything, stronger and more relaxed. They appeared to be able to cope with the stresses and strains of life, and, if anything, they seemed to enjoy social functions more than the smoker. They certainly had more sparkle and zest than the smokers.

I started talking to ex-smokers. Up to this point I had regarded ex-smokers as having been forced to give up smoking for health and money reasons and that they were always secretly longing for a cigarette. A few did say "You get the odd pangs, but they are so few and far between it wasn't worth bothering about". But most said something like "Miss it, you must be joking. I have never felt better in my life."

Talking to ex-smokers exploded another doubt that I had always had in my mind. I had thought that there was an inherent weakness in me and it suddenly dawned on me that all smokers go through this private nightmare. Basically I said to myself "Millions of people are stopping now and leading perfectly happy lives. I didn't need to do it before I started and I could remember having to work so hard to get used to the filthy things, so why do I need to do it now?" In any event I didn't enjoy smoking, I hated the whole filthy ritual and I do not want to spend the rest of my life being the slave of this disgusting weed.

I then said to myself: "Allen, WHETHER YOU LIKE IT OR NOT YOU HAVE SMOKED YOUR LAST CIGARETTE".

I knew right from that point that I would never smoke again. I wasn't expecting it to be easy, in fact just the reverse. I fully believed that I was in for months of black depression and that I would spend the rest of my life having the occasional pang. Instead absolute bliss right from the start.

It took me a long time to work out why it had been so easy and why this time I hadn't suffered those terrifying withdrawal pangs. The reason was that they do not exist. It is the doubt and uncertainty that causes the pangs. The beautiful truth is "IT IS EASY TO STOP SMOKING". It is only the indecision and moping about it that makes it difficult. Even while they are addicted to nicotine, smokers can go relatively long periods at certain times in their lives without bothering about it. It is only when you want one, but can't have one, that you suffer.

Therefore the key to making it easy is, to make it certain and final. Not to hope but to know you have kicked it and then having made the decision. Never to doubt or question it, in fact just the reverse – always rejoice about it.

We have a slight chicken and egg situation. If you can make it certain from the start, it will be easy. But how can you make it certain from the start, until you know it is going to be easy? This is why the rest of the book is necessary. There are certain essential points and it is necessary to get them clearly in your mind before you start. They are:

1 To realise that you can achieve it. There is nothing different about you and that the only person that can make you smoke that next cigarette is you.

2 That there is absolutely nothing to give up, on the contrary, there are enormous positive gains to be made. I do not only mean you will be healthier and richer, I mean you will enjoy the good times more and be less miserable during the bad times.

3 Get it clearly in your head, there is no such thing as one cigarette! It is a drug addiction and a chain reaction. By moaning about the odd cigarette, you will only be punishing yourself needlessly.

4 See the whole business of smoking, not as it is sold to you i.e. A sociable habit, that might injure you, but as it actually is: drug addiction and the No. 1 killer poison in Western society. Face up to the fact that whether you like it or not – YOU HAVE GOT THE DISEASE. It will not go away because you put your head back into the sand. Remember like all crippling diseases, it not only lasts for life but gets worse and worse, and that the easiest time to cure it is *now*.

5 Separate the disease i.e. the chemical addiction, from the frame of mind of being a smoker or a non-smoker. All smokers if given the opportunity to go back to the time before they became hooked, would jump at that opportunity. Get it into your head, you have that opportunity today! Don't even think about it as giving-up smoking. When you have made the final decision that you have smoked your last cigarette you will already be a non-smoker. A smoker is one of those poor wretches who has to go through life

destroying himself with cigarettes. A non-smoker is someone that doesn't. Once you have made that final decision you have already achieved your object. Rejoice in the fact, do not sit moping waiting for the chemical addiction to go. Get out and enjoy life right from square one. Life is marvellous even when you are addicted to nicotine and each day it will get better.

The key to making it easy to give up smoking is firstly to be so certain in your mind that you will succeed in abstaining completely during the withdrawal period (maximum 3 weeks) and, if you are in the correct frame of mind, you will find it ridiculously easy.

By this stage, if you have opened your mind as I requested at the beginning, you will already have decided you are going to stop. You should now have a feeling of excitement like a dog straining at the lead being unable to wait to get the poison out of your system.

If you have a feeling of doom and gloom, it will be due to one of the following:

1   Something has not gelled in your mind. Re-read the above 5 points and ask yourself if you believe them to be true. If you doubt any point, re-read the appropriate sections in the book.
2   You fear failure itself. Do not worry, just read on. You will not be able to help but succeed. The whole business of smoking is like a confidence trick on a gigantic scale. Intelligent people fall for confidence tricks, but it is only a fool that having once found out about the trick goes on kidding himself.
3   You agree with everything but you are still miserable. Don't be! Open your eyes, something marvellous is happening, you are about to escape from the prison.

It is essential to start with the correct frame of mind i.e. Isn't it marvellous I am a non-smoker?

All we have to do now is to keep you in that frame of mind during the withdrawal period and the next few chapters deal with specific points to enable you to stay in that frame of mind during that time. After the withdrawal period you won't have to think that way. You will think that way automatically and the only mystery in your life will be: "It is so obvious, why couldn't I see it before?" However two important warnings:

1   Delay your attempt to decide on your last cigarette until you have finished the book.

2   I have mentioned several times, a withdrawal period of up to 3 weeks. This can cause misunderstanding. Firstly you may subconsciously feel that you have to suffer for 3 weeks. You don't. Secondly avoid the trap of thinking "I have just got to somehow abstain for 3 weeks and then I will be free". Avoid this trap, nothing will actually happen after 3 weeks. You won't suddenly feel like a non-smoker. Non-smokers do not feel any different to smokers. If you are moping about it during the 3 weeks, in all probability you will still be moping about it after the 3 weeks. What I am saying is, if you can start right from point one by saying: "I am never going to smoke again, isn't it marvellous", after 3 weeks all temptation will go. Whereas if you say "If only I can survive 3 weeks without a cigarette", you will be dying for a cigarette after the 3 weeks are up. (Unintentional pun.)

33

The Withdrawal Period

For up to three weeks after your last cigarette you may be subjected to withdrawal pangs. These consist of two quite separate factors:

1. The withdrawal pangs of nicotine. That empty insecure feeling like a hunger which smokers identify as something to do with their hands.
2. The psychological trigger mechanism of relieving the above pangs to coincide with certain events e.g. a telephone conversation.

It is the failure to understand and to differentiate between these two distinct factors that make it so difficult for smokers under the Willpower Method to achieve success and it's also the reason that many smokers that do achieve it fall into the trap again.

Although the withdrawal pangs from nicotine cause no physical pain, do not underestimate their power. We talk of "hunger pains" but if we go without food for a day, there may be "tummy rumblings" but there is no physical pain. Even so it is a powerful force and we are likely to become very irritable when deprived of food. It is similar when our body is craving nicotine. The difference is our body needs food but it doesn't need poison and with the right frame of mind the actual withdrawal pains are easily overcome and disappear very quickly.

If smokers under the Willpower Method can abstain for a few days, the actual craving for nicotine soon disappears. It is this second factor that causes the difficulty. The smoker has got into the habit of relieving his withdrawal pangs at certain times or occasions which causes an association of ideas e.g. "I cannot enjoy a drink without a cigarette". It may be easier to understand the effect by use of an example.

You may have a car for a few years and let's say the indicator lever is on the left of the steering column. On your next car it is on the right (the law of sod). You know it is on the right but for a couple of weeks you put the windscreen wipers on whenever you want to indicate.

It is similar with giving up smoking. During the early days of the withdrawal period at certain times this trigger operation will operate in the form of "I want a cigarette". It is essential to counter the brain-washing right from square one and these automatic triggers will quickly disappear. Under the Willpower Method, because the smoker believes he is making a sacrifice, is moping about it, waiting for the urge to smoke to go, far from removing these trigger mechanisms he is actually increasing them.

A common example is the cigarette during or after a meal particularly at a restaurant with friends. The smoker is already miserable because he is being deprived of his cigarette. His friends light-up and he feels even more deprived. Now he is not enjoying the meal, or what should be a pleasant social occasion. Because of his association of the cigarette with the meal and the social occasion he is now suffering a triple blow and the brainwashing is actually being increased. If he is resolute and can hold out long enough, he eventually accepts his lot and gets on with his life. However, part of the brainwashing remains and I think the second most pathetic thing about smoking is the smoker who has given up for health or money reasons and, even after several years, still craves a cigarette on certain occasions. He is pining over an illusion that only exists in his mind and is needlessly torturing himself.

Even under my method I find this aspect the most common failing. The ex-smoker tends to regard the cigarette as a sort of placebo or sugar pill. He thinks:

"I know the cigarette actually does nothing for me, but if I think it does, on certain occasions it will be a help to me."

A sugar pill, although giving no actual physical help, can be a powerful psychological aid to relieve genuine symptoms and is therefore a benefit. However the cigarette is not a sugar pill, it actually creates the symptoms that it relieves and after a while ceases even to completely relieve these symptoms; the pill is causing the disease and quite apart from that it also happens to be the No. 1 killer poison in Western society.

You may find it easier to understand the effect when related to non-smokers or a smoker that has quit for several years. Take the case where a wife loses her husband. It is quite common at such times for a smoker, with the best intentions in mind, to say:

"Have a cigarette, it will help calm you down."

If the cigarette is accepted, it will not have a calming effect because the woman is not addicted to nicotine and there are no withdrawal pangs to relieve. At best all it will do is give a momentary psychological boost. As soon as the cigarette is extinguished, the original tragedy is still there. In fact it will be increased because the woman is now suffering withdrawal pangs and her choice is now either to suffer them or relieve them by smoking another cigarette and start the chain of misery. All the cigarette will have done is to give a momentary psychological boost. The same effect could have been achieved a dozen different ways by offering a word of comfort or a drink. Many non-smokers and ex-smokers have become addicted to the weed as a result of such occasions.

It is essential to counter the brainwashing right from the start. Get it clearly into your head, you don't need the cigarette and you are only torturing yourself by continuing to regard it as some sort of prop or boost. There is no need to be miserable. Cigarettes do not make meals or social occasions, they ruin them and even whilst you are addicted to nicotine you can enjoy meals and life.

Also remember the smokers at that meal are not smoking because they are enjoying the cigarette, they are smoking because they have got to. They are drug addicts! They cannot enjoy the meal or life without it.

It will also help to remove the concept of the smoking habit being pleasurable in itself. Many smokers think "If only there was a clean cigarette". There are clean cigarettes. Any smoker that has tried Herbal cigarettes soon finds out they are a waste of time. Get it clearly into your mind the only reason you have been smoking that cigarette is to get the nicotine. Once you have got rid of the craving for nicotine you will have no more need to stick a cigarette in your mouth than you would in your ear, so stop kidding yourself otherwise.

Whether the pang is due to actual withdrawal symptoms (the empty feeling) or a trigger mechanism, accept it. The physical pain is non-existent and with the right frame of mind cigarettes become no problem. Do not worry about it. The feeling itself isn't bad. It is the association with wanting a cigarette and then feeling denied that causes the problem.

Instead of moping about it, do just the opposite. Just say to yourself, "I know what it is, it's the withdrawal pangs from nicotine. That's what smokers suffer all their lives and that's what keeps them smoking. Non-smokers do not suffer these pangs. It is another of the many evils of this drug. Isn't it marvellous I am purging this evil from my body."

In other words for the next three weeks you will have a slight trauma inside your body i.e. the withdrawal pangs from nicotine but, for the next 3 weeks and for the rest of your life, something marvellous will be happening. You will be ridding yourself of this awful disease. Use that bonus, it will more than outweigh the slight trauma and that way you will actually enjoy the withdrawal pangs. They will become moments of pleasure.

Think of the whole business of stopping as an exciting game. Think of the nicotine monster as a sort of tape worm inside your stomach. You have got to starve him for 3 weeks and he is going to try to trick you into keeping him alive by lighting a cigarette.

At times he will try to make you miserable. At times you will be off guard. Someone may offer you a cigarette and you may have forgotten you have stopped. There is a slight feeling of deprivation when you remember. Be prepared for these traps in advance. Whatever the reason for the temptation, get it into your mind that it is only there because of this monster inside your body and that every time you resist the temptation is another mortal blow in the battle.

Whatever you do, don't try to forget about smoking. This is one of the things that causes smokers using the Willpower Method to have hours of depression. They try to get through each day hoping eventually that they'll just forget about it.

It is like not being able to sleep. The more you worry about it, the harder it becomes.

In any event you won't be able to forget about it. For the first few days the "little monster" will keep reminding you and in any event you won't be able to avoid it. While there are still smokers about you will have constant reminders and the extensive cigarette promotions will make it impossible to forget.

The point is you have no need to forget. There is nothing bad happening, something marvellous is happening. Even if you are thinking about it a thousand times a day, SAVOUR EACH MOMENT. REMIND YOURSELF HOW MARVELLOUS IT IS TO BE FREE AGAIN. THE SHEER JOY OF NOT HAVING TO CHOKE YOURSELF ANY MORE.

As I have said, you will find that the pangs become moments of pleasure and you will be surprised how quickly you will then forget about it.

Whatever you do – DO NOT DOUBT YOUR DECISION. Once you start to doubt, it's a cause and effect situation, you will start to mope and it will get worse. Instead use the moment as a boost. If the cause was depression remind yourself that's what the cigarette is doing to you. If it was being offered one by a friend, take pride in saying "I'm happy to say I do not need them any more". That will hurt him but when he sees that it isn't bothering you he will be half way to joining you.

Remember you had very powerful reasons for stopping in the first place. Remind yourself of the £X,000 that one cigarette will cost you and whether you really want to go risking those fearful diseases. Above all remember the feeling is only temporary and each moment is a moment nearer to your goal.

Some smokers fear that they will have to spend the rest of their lives reversing the "automatic triggers". In other words, they believe that they will have to go through life kidding themselves that they don't really need a cigarette by the use of psychology. This is not so. Psychology is where the optimist sees the bottle half full and the pessimist sees it as half empty. In the case of smoking, the bottle is empty and the smoker sees it as full. Remember, it is the smoker who has been brainwashed. Once you start telling yourself that you don't need to smoke, in a very short time, you won't even need to say it. It will be that way because the beautiful truth is . . . Not only do you not need to smoke (it's the last thing you need to do), make sure it's not THE LAST THING YOU DO!

34

Just One Puff

This is the undoing of many smokers who try to stop under the Willpower Method. They will go through three or four days and then have the odd cigarette or a few puffs or just one to tide them over. They do not realise the devastating effect this has to their morale.

For most smokers that first puff doesn't taste good and this gives their conscious minds a boost. They think "Good, that wasn't enjoyable, I am losing the urge to smoke".

In fact the reverse is the case. Get it clearly into your mind – THEY NEVER WERE ENJOYABLE! Enjoyment wasn't the reason you smoked. If smokers smoked for enjoyment, they'd never smoke more than one cigarette.

The only reason you have been smoking is to feed that little monster. Just think you have starved him for four days, how precious that one cigarette or just the puff must have been to him. You are not aware of it in your conscious mind but the fix your body received will be communicated to your subconscious mind and all the sound preparation you have made will be undermined. There will be a little voice at the back of your mind saying "In spite of all the logic they are precious, I want another one".

That little puff has two damaging effects:

1 It keeps the "little monster" alive in your body.
2 What's worse, it keeps the "big monster" alive in the mind. If you had the last puff it will be easier to have the next one.
   Remember just one cigarette is how people get onto smoking in the first place.

35

Will it be Harder for Me?

The number of combinations that affect each individual smoker regarding how hard or easy it will be are infinite. To start with each of us has his own character, our type of work, the state of our personal lives, the timing etc.

Certain professions make it harder than others but providing the brainwashing is removed it doesn't have to be so. A few individual examples will help.

It tends to be particularly difficult for members of the medical profession. We think it should be easier for Doctors because they are more aware of the effects to ill-health and are seeing daily evidence of it. Although this provides greater reasons for stopping it doesn't make it any easier to do so. The reasons are:

1　The constant knowledge of the bad health effects creates fear which is one of the occasions we need to relieve our withdrawal pangs.
2　A Doctor's work is exceedingly stressful and he is usually not able to relieve the additional stress of withdrawal pangs whilst he is working.
3　He has the additional stress of guilt. He feels that he should be setting an example to the rest of the population. This puts more pressure on him and increases the feeling of deprivation.

During his hard-earned breaks, when the normal stress is momentarily relieved, how precious that cigarette becomes when he eventually relieves his withdrawal pangs. This is another form of casual smoking and applies to any situation where the smoker is forced to abstain for lengthy periods. Under the Willpower Method the smoker is miserable because he is being deprived. He is not enjoying the break or the cup of tea or coffee that goes with it. His sense of loss is therefore greatly increased and, because of the association of ideas, the cigarette gets credit for the total situation. However, if you can first remove the brainwashing and stop moping about the cigarette, the break and the cup of tea can still be enjoyed even while the body is craving nicotine.

Another difficult situation is boredom particularly when it is combined with periods of stress. Typical examples are drivers or housewives with young children. The work is stressful and yet much of the work is monotonous. During an attempt to stop under the Willpower Method, the housewife has long periods to mope about her "loss" which increases the feeling of depression.

Again this can be easily overcome if the frame of mind is correct. Do not worry that you are continually reminded that you have stopped smoking. Use those moments to rejoice in the fact that you are ridding yourself of the evil monster. If you keep a positive frame of mind, these pangs can become moments of pleasure.

A situation which is less easy to overcome are professions involving inspiration such as for artists and writers who find it very difficult to concentrate during the withdrawal period. The answer here is to accept the situation. If you broke your leg you wouldn't expect to have to carry on as if nothing had happened. Nicotine addiction is far worse than a broken leg, it will last the rest of your life, will cost you a fortune, shorten your life and eventually make it impossible to concentrate. Give yourself a reasonable chance of a cure. Let the work suffer during the withdrawal period or better still try to pick a suitable time to make your attempt e.g. during a holiday.

36

The Main Reasons for Failure

There are two main reasons for failure. The first is the influence of other smokers. At a weak moment or during a social occasion, somebody will light up. I have already dealt with this topic at length. Use that moment to remind yourself that there is no such thing as one cigarette. Rejoice in the fact that you have broken the chain. Remember that the smoker envies you, and feel sorry for him. Believe me he needs your pity.

The other main reason for failure is having a bad day. Get it clearly in your mind before you start that, whether you are a smoker or a non-smoker, there are good days and bad days. Life is a matter of relativity and you cannot have ups without having downs.

The problem is that during the Willpower Method of stopping, as soon as the smoker has a bad day he starts moping for a cigarette and all he does is make a bad day worse.

Keep it clearly in your mind that the non-smoker is better equipped not only physically but also mentally to cope with the stresses and strains of life.

If you have a bad day during the withdrawal period just take it on the chin, remind yourself that you had bad days when you smoked (otherwise you wouldn't have decided to stop) and instead of moping about it, do the opposite, say to yourself something like, "O.K. today's not so good, but smoking is not going to cure it, tomorrow will be better and at least I have got a marvellous bonus at the moment, I have kicked that awful cigarette habit.

Remember a positive mental approach.

37

Substitutes

Substitutes include, chewing gum, eating sweets, peppermints, herbal cigarettes, pills. DO NOT USE ANY OF THEM. They make it harder not easier. If you do get a pang and use a substitute, it will prolong the pang and make it harder. What you are really saying is "I need to smoke or fill the void" It will be like giving into the first high-jacker or the tantrums of a child. It will just keep the pangs coming and prolong the torture. In any event the substitutes will not relieve the pangs. Your craving is for nicotine not food. All it will do is keep you thinking about smoking. Remember this:

1   There is no substitute for nicotine.
2   You do not need one, it is not food, it is poison. When the pangs come remind yourself that it is smokers that suffer withdrawal pangs not non-smokers and see it as another evil of the drug, see it as the death of a dying monster.
3   Remember cigarettes create the void, they do not fill it; the quicker you teach your brain that you do not need to do it, or anything else in its place, the sooner you will be free.

In particular avoid chewing gum or any other product that contains nicotine. The theory is that you stop smoking and that while you break the habit you keep nicotine in your body and therefore do not suffer bad withdrawal pangs. In practice it actually makes it harder to stop for this reason. In the case of cigarettes the habit is feeding withdrawal symptoms. Nicotine give you no actual benefit you only smoke to relieve the actual withdrawal pangs and the habit dies with the pangs. The withdrawal pangs from nicotine are so slight that there is no actual need to relieve them. The main problem in smoking, as I have already explained, is not the physical addiction but the *mental* brainwashing. All that nicotine chewing gum does is to prolong the chemical addiction which in turn just prolongs the mental addiction.

There are many ex-smokers who are now hooked on nicotine chewing gum. There are also many people hooked on the gum who are still smoking.

Do not kid yourself by thinking the gum tastes awful, just remember so did that first cigarette.

38

Should I Avoid Temptation Situations?

I have been categoric in my advice so far and would ask you to treat this advice as instructions, rather than suggestions. I am categoric firstly because there are sound, practical reasons for my advice and secondly because those reasons have been backed up by thousands of case studies.

On the question of whether or not to try to avoid temptation situations during the withdrawal period, I regret that I cannot be categoric. Each smoker will need to decide for himself. However I can make what I hope will be helpful suggestions.

I repeat that it is fear that keeps us smoking all our lives and this fear consists of two distinct phases:

1   How can I survive without a cigarette?
    This fear is that panic feeling that smokers get when they are out late at night and their cigarettes begin to run out. The fear isn't actually caused by withdrawal pangs but is the psychological fear of dependency – that you cannot survive without a cigarette. It actually reaches its height when you are smoking your last cigarette and at that time your withdrawal pangs are at their lowest.

    It is the fear of the unknown the same sort of fear that people have when they are learning to dive, the diving board is 1 ft high but seems to be 6 ft high. The water is 6 ft deep but appears to be 1 ft deep. It takes courage to launch yourself. You are convinced you are going to smash your head. The launching is the hardest part. If you can find the courage to do so, the rest is easy.

    This explains why many otherwise strong-willed smokers have either never attempted to stop or can only survive a few hours when they do. In fact there are some smokers on about 20-a-day, who, when they decide to stop, actually smoke their next cigarette quicker than if they had not decided to stop. The decision causes panic which is stressful. This is one of the occasions when the brain triggers, "have a cigarette" but now you can't have one, you are being deprived – more stress – the trigger starts again – quickly the fuse blows and you light-up.

Don't worry, that panic is just psychological. It is the fear that you are dependent. The beautiful truth is that you are not, even when you are still addicted to nicotine. Do not panic, just trust me and launch yourself.

2   The second type of fear is longer term i.e. the fear that certain situations in the future will either be not enjoyable without a cigarette or whether the ex-smoker will be able to cope with a trauma without the cigarette. Don't worry, if you can launch yourself you will find the opposite to be the case.

The avoidance of temptation itself falls into two main categories.

1   I will keep my cigarettes available although I will not smoke them but I feel more confident knowing they are there.

I find the failure rate with people that do this is far higher than with people who discard them. I believe this is mainly due to the fact that if you have a bad moment during the withdrawal period, it is easy to light one up. Whereas if you have the indignity of having to go out and buy a packet you are more likely to overcome the temptation and in any event the pang will probably have passed before you get to the tobacconists.

However, I believe the main reason for the higher failure rate in these cases is that the smoker does not feel completely committed to stopping in the first place. Remember the two essentials to succeed are:

1   Certainty.
2   Isn't it marvellous I do not need to smoke anymore.

In either case why on earth do you need cigarettes. If you still feel the need to keep cigarettes on your person, I would suggest that you re-read the book first. It means that something hasn't gelled.

2   The other form of avoidance of temptation is usually either "should I avoid stressful situations" e.g. avoid going to the dentist, or should I avoid social occasions e.g. weddings etc. during the withdrawal period?

My advice to the stress situation is yes, try to avoid them. There is no sense in putting undue pressure on yourself.

In the case of social events my advice is the reverse. No, go out and enjoy yourself straight away. You do not need cigarettes even whilst you are addicted to nicotine. Go to the party and rejoice in the fact that you do not have to smoke. It will quickly prove to you the beautiful truth that it is so much better without them and just think how much better it will be when that little monster has left your body together with all that poison.

39

The Moment of Revelation

The moment of revelation usually takes place about three weeks after a smoker stops. The sky appears to become brighter and it is the moment when the brainwashing ends completely. When, instead of telling yourself you do not need to smoke, you suddenly realise that it is true, the last thread is broken, and you know that you can enjoy the rest of your life never needing to smoke again. It is also usually from this point that you start looking at other smokers as objects of pity.

Smokers using the Willpower Method do not normally achieve this moment because although they are glad to be ex-smokers they go through life actually believing they are making a sacrifice.

The more chronic you were, the more marvellous this moment is and it lasts a lifetime.

I consider I have been very fortunate in this life and had some marvellous moments but the most wonderful of all was that moment of revelation. With all the other highlights of my life, although I can remember they were happy times, I can never recapture the actual feeling. I can never get over the actual joy of not having to smoke anymore. If ever I am feeling low and need a boost nowadays, I just think how lovely it is not to be hooked on that awful weed. Half the people that contact me after they have kicked the weed say exactly the same thing, that it was the most marvellous event of their lives. Ah! What pleasure you have to come!

40

That Last Cigarette

Having decided your timing, you are now ready to smoke that last cigarette. Before you do so just check on the two essentials:

1 Do you feel certain of success?
2 Your frame of mind. Have you a feeling of doom and gloom or a feeling of excitement that you are about to achieve something marvellous.

If you have any doubts re-read the book first.

When you feel quite ready, smoke that last cigarette. Do it alone and do not smoke it subconsciously. Concentrate on every puff, concentrate on the taste and smell, concentrate on the cancerous fumes going into your lungs, concentrate on the poisons gunging up your arteries and veins, concentrate on the nicotine going into your body and, when you put it out, just think how marvellous it will be not to have to go on doing it. The joy of being freed from this slavery. Its like coming out of a world of black shadows into a world of sunshine.

41

A Final Warning

All smokers given the chance of going back to the time before they became hooked, with the knowledge they have now, would opt never to have started. Many of the smokers who consult me are convinced that if I could only help them stop they would never dream of smoking again, and yet thousands of smokers successfully kick the habit for many years leading perfectly happy lives, only to get trapped again in the future.

I trust this book will help you to find it relatively easy to stop smoking. But be warned, smokers that find it easy to stop find it easy to start again.

DO NOT FALL FOR THIS TRAP

No matter how long you have stopped and how confident you feel that you will never become hooked again, make it a rule of life just not to try one for any reason. Resist the millions of pounds that the tobacco companies spend on promotion and remember they are pushing the No. 1 killer drug and poison. You wouldn't be tempted to try heroin and cigarettes kill hundreds of thousands more people in Western society than heroin.

Remember that first cigarette will do nothing for you. You will have no withdrawal pangs to relieve and it will taste awful. What it will do is to put nicotine into your body and as soon as you put it out a little voice at the back of your mind will be saying "You want another one". Then you have got the choice of being miserable for a while or starting the whole filthy chain again.

42

Help the Poor Smoker Left on the Sinking Ship

Smokers are getting into a panic nowadays. They sense that there is a change in society. Smoking is now accepted as an unsociable habit, even by the smoker himself. They also sense that the whole thing is coming to an end. Millions of smokers are now stopping and all smokers are conscious of the fact.

Everytime a smoker leaves the sinking ship, the ones left on it feel more miserable. The reason that it was such a sociable habit in the first place is that every smoker instinctively knows that it is ridiculous to pay good money for dried leaves rolled up in paper, setting light to it and to breathe cancer-triggering tar into your lungs. If you still don't think it is silly try sticking a burning cigarette in your ear and ask yourself whats the difference. Just one. You cannot get the nicotine that way. If you stop sticking them in your mouth you won't need the nicotine.

Smokers cannot find a rational reason for doing it, but if there is someone else doing it they do not feel quite so silly.

Smokers blatantly lie about their habit, not only to you but to themselves. They have to. The brainwashing is essential to retain some self-respect. They feel the need to justify their habit, not only to themselves but to non-smokers. They are, therefore, forever advertising the illusory advantages of smoking.

If a smoker stops on the Willpower Method, he still feels deprived and tends to become a moaner. "Oh I'd love a cigarette". All this does is to confirm to other smokers how right they are to keep smoking.

If the ex-smoker succeeds in really kicking the habit, he tends just to be grateful that he no longer has to go through life choking himself or wasting money. But because it is negative, because he is not doing it and has no need to justify himself, he doesn't sit there saying how marvellous it is not to be smoking. He will only do that if he is asked and smokers won't ask that question, they wouldn't like the answer.

Remember it is fear that keeps them smoking and they would rather keep their heads in the sand.

The only time they ask that question is when it is time to stop.

Help the smoker. Remove these fears. Tell him how marvellous it is not to have to go through life choking yourself. How lovely it is to be able to wake up in the morning feeling fit and healthy instead of having to start wheezing and coughing. How wonderful it is to be free of slavery, to be able to enjoy the whole of your life, to be rid of those awful black shadows.

Or better still get him to read the book.

It is essential not to try to belittle the smoker by indicating that he is polluting the atmosphere or is in some way unclean. There is a common conception that the ex-smoker is the worst in this respect. I believe this conception has some substance and I think this is due to the Willpower Method of stopping. Because the ex-smoker, although pleased that he has kicked the habit, still retains part of the brainwashing, part of him still believes that he has made a sacrifice. He feels vulnerable and the natural defensive mechanism is to attack the smoker. This may help the ex-smoker but it does nothing to help the smoker. All it does is put his back up, makes him feel even more wretched and consequently makes his need for a cigarette even greater.

Although this change in Society's attitude to smoking i.e. from a socially acceptable habit to a filthy disgusting habit, is the main reason why millions of smokers are kicking the habit, it doesn't make it easier for them to do so. In fact it makes it a great deal harder. Most smokers believe they are stopping nowadays mainly for health reasons. This is not strictly true. Although the enormous health risk is obviously the chief, rational benefit of quitting the habit, smokers have been killing themselves for years and it made not the slightest difference. The main reason that smokers are actually stopping is because society is beginning to treat the habit as what it actually is: filthy drug addiction. The enjoyment was always an illusion and this attitude removes this illusion so that the smoker is left with nothing.

The recent complete ban on London tube trains is a classic example. The smoker either takes the attitude:

"O.K. if I cannot smoke on the train I will find another means of travel", which does no good but merely loses London Transport valuable revenue.

or he says:

"Fine, it will help me cut down on my smoking" the result of this is that instead of smoking one or two cigarettes on the train, neither of which he would have enjoyed, he abstains for an hour. But during this enforced period of abstinence, not only will he mentally be deprived and waiting for his reward, but his body will have physically been craving nicotine – and oh how precious that cigarette will be when he is eventually allowed to light up.

In fact, usually these enforced abstinences do not actually cut-down the intake because the smoker just indulges himself in more cigarettes when he is eventually allowed to smoke. All it does is to ingrain into the smoker's mind how precious the cigarette is and how dependent he is upon them. I think the most insidious aspect of this enforced abstinence is our society's attitude to pregnant women. We allow unfortunate teen-agers to be bombarded with massive advertising which gets them hooked in the first place. Then, at what is probably the most stressful period in their lives, when in their deluded mind they need a cigarette most of all, the medical profession then blackmail them into giving up because of the harm they are causing the baby. Many are unable to do so and are forced, through no fault of their own, to suffer a guilt complex the rest of their lives. Many of them succeed and are pleased to do so thinking, "Fine, I will do this for the baby and after nine months I will be cured anyway". Then comes the most stressful period of their lives. The pain and fear of labour, followed by the biggest "High" of their lives. The pain and fear is over and the beautiful, new baby has arrived. These are the very occasions when the old trigger mechanism comes into operation. Part of the brainwashing is still there and, almost before the cord has been cut, the girl has a cigarette in her mouth. The elation of the occasion blocks her mind from the foul taste. She has no intention of becoming hooked again. "Just the one cigarette." Too late! She is already hooked. Nicotine has already gone into her body again. The old craving will start and, even if she doesn't become hooked again straight away, the post-natal depression will probably catch her out.

It is strange that although heroin addicts are criminals in law, our society's attitude is quite rightly "What can we do to help the pathetic individuals". Let us adopt the same attitude to the poor smoker. He is not smoking because he wants to but because he thinks he has got to, and, unlike the heroin addict, he usually has to suffer years and years of mental and physical torture. We always say a quick death is better than a slow one, so do not envy the poor smoker, he needs your PITY!

43

Advice to Non-Smokers

A. TO HELP GET YOUR SMOKING FRIENDS OR
RELATIVES TO READ THIS BOOK.

i. First study the contents of this book yourself and try to put yourself in the place of the smoker.

ii. Do not try to force him to read this book, or to stop smoking by telling him he is ruining his health or wasting his money. He already knows this better than you do. Smokers smoke not because they enjoy it or because they want to, they only tell themselves and other people this in order to retain self-respect. They smoke because they feel dependant on cigarettes, because they think the cigarette relaxes them, gives them courage and confidence, that life will never be enjoyable without a cigarette. If you try to force a smoker out of it he feels like a trapped animal and wants his cigarette even more. This will only turn him into a secret smoker and in his mind the cigarette will become even more precious (see chapter 26).

iii. Instead, concentrate on the other side of the coin, get him into the company of other heavy smokers who have kicked the habit (there are 10 million of them in Britain alone). Get them to tell the smoker how they, too, thought they were hooked for life and how much better life is as a non-smoker.

iv. Once you have got him believing that he can stop, his mind will start opening. Then start explaining the delusion created by withdrawal pangs, that not only are the cigarettes not giving him a boost but it is they that are destroying his confidence and making him irritable and unrelaxed.

v. He should now be ready to read this book himself. He will be expecting to read pages and pages about lung cancer, heart diseases etc.; just explain that the approach is completely different and that this is just a small fraction of the material.

B. TO HELP DURING WITHDRAWAL PERIOD

i. Whether the ex-smoker is suffering or not assume that he is. Do not try to minimise his suffering by telling him it is easy to stop, he can do that himself. Instead keep telling him how proud you are. How much better he is looking, how much sweeter he smells, how much easier his breathing is. It is particularly important to keep doing this. When a smoker makes an attempt to stop, the euphoria of the attempt and the attention he gets from friends and colleagues can help him along. However they tend to forget quickly, so does the smoker, so keep that praise going.

ii. Because he is not talking about the smoking, you may think he has forgotten about it and not like to remind him. Usually it is the complete opposite in the Willpower Method as the ex-smoker tends to be obsessed with nothing else. So do not be frightened to bring the subject up, keep praising him; he will tell you if he doesn't want you to remind him.

iii. Go out of your way to relieve him of pressures during the withdrawal period. Try to think of ways of making his life interesting and enjoyable.

iv. This can also be a trying period for non-smokers. If one member of a group is irritable, this can cause general misery all round. So anticipate this if the ex-smoker is feeling irritable. He may well take it out on you, do not retaliate; it is at this time that he needs your praise and sympathy the most. If you are feeling irritable yourself, try not to show it.

v. One of the tricks I used to play when trying to give up with the Willpower Method was to get into such a tantrum, hoping that my wife or friends would say, "I cannot bear to see you suffering like this. For goodness sake have a cigarette". The smoker then does not lose face as it is not him "giving-in" – he has been instructed. If the ex-smoker uses this ploy, on no account encourage him to smoke. Instead say, "If that is what cigarettes do to you, thank goodness you will soon be free. How marvellous, you had the courage and sense to give up".

FINALE

Help End This Scandal

In my opinion cigarette smoking is the biggest scandal in Western society including nuclear weapons.

Surely the very basis of civilisation, the reason that the human species has advanced so far, is that we are capable of communicating our knowledge and experiences, not only to each other, but to future generations. Even the lower species find it necessary to warn their off-spring of the pitfalls in life.

With nuclear weapons, if they do not go off, there is no problem. The people that advocate nuclear policy can carry on saying smugly, "They are keeping the peace". If they do go off, they will solve the smoking problem and every other problem and an added bonus for the politicians is that there will be nobody around to say "You were wrong" (I wonder if this is why they take the former option).

However, much as I disagree with the nuclear weapon thinking, at least those decisions are made in good faith, taken in the genuine belief that they help mankind, whereas with smoking, they know the true facts. Maybe during the last war they genuinely believed that cigarettes gave you courage and confidence whereas today the auth-orities know it is a fallacy? Just watch the cigarette adverts nowadays. They make no claim of relaxation or giving pleasure. The only claim they make are in size or the quality of the tobacco. Why should we be worried about the size and quality of a poison?

The sheer hypocrisy is incredible. Our Government force us to wear seat belts to save a few hundred lives. As a society we get uptight about glue sniffing and heroin addiction. Our Government are quite rightly debating life sentences for heroin pushers. Compared to cigarette smoking, these problems are mere pimples in our society. Sixty per cent of the population have been addicted to nicotine and most of them spend the bulk of their pocket money on cigarettes. Tens of thousands of people have their lives ruined every year because they become hooked. It is by far the biggest killer in Western society and yet the biggest vested interest is our own Treasury. They make £5,000,000,000 every year out of the misery of nicotine addicts and the tobacco empires are allowed to spend £100,000,000 per year advertising the filth.

How clever that cigarette companies can print that Health Warning on the packet, and that our Government can spend a pittance on T.V. campaigns involving cancer scares, bad breath, and legs being chopped off and then justify themselves morally by saying, "We have warned you of the danger. It is your choice". The smoker doesn't have the choice any more than the heroin addict does. Smokers do not decide to become hooked; they are lured into a subtle trap. If smokers had the choice, the only smokers tomorrow morning would be the youngsters starting out believing they could stop any time they wanted to.

Why the phoney standards; why are heroin addicts seen as criminals in law and yet can register as addicts and get free heroin and proper medical treatment to help get off it? Just try registering as a nicotine addict. You cannot even get them at cost. You have to pay three times the true value and every Budget Day you will be screwed further by the Government. As if the smoker hadn't got troubles enough!

If you go to your doctor for help, he will either tell you "Stop doing it, it's killing you" which you already know, thats why you went to him. Or he will prescribe a chewing gum which will cost you a prescription fee of, perhaps, £11 and actually contains the drug you are trying to kick.

These scare campaigns do not help smokers to stop, they actually make it harder. All it does is to frighten them, which makes them want to smoke even more. It doesn't even prevent teenagers becoming hooked. Teenagers know cigarettes kill you, but they know one cigarette will not do it. Because the habit is so prevalent, sooner or later, the teenager, through social pressures or curiosity, will try just one cigarette. And because it tastes so awful, he will probably become hooked.

Why do we allow this scandal to go on? Why doesn't our government come out with a proper campaign? Why don't they tell us that it is a drug and a No. 1. killer poison and that it does not relax you and give you confidence but that it is destroying your nerves and that it can take just one cigarette to become hooked?

I remember reading H. G. Wells' *The Time Machine*. The book described an incident in the distant future in which a man had fallen into a river. His companions merely sat around the bank like cattle, oblivious to his cries of desperation. I found that incident inhuman and very disturbing. I find the general apathy of our society to the smoking problem to be very similar. We allow darts tournaments to be televised during peak viewing hours, usually sponsored by tobacco companies. There is a cry of "one hundred and eighty". The player is then shown lighting a cigarette. Imagine the furore if the tournament were being sponsored by the Mafia, that the player was a heroin addict, and was shown injecting himself.

Why do we allow society to continue to take physically and mentally healthy young teenagers, youngsters whose lives are complete before they start smoking, and allow them to be submitted to paying through the nose for the rest of their lives, just for the privilege of destroying themselves mentally and physically in a lifetime of slavery – a lifetime of filth and disease.

You may feel that I over dramatise the facts. Not so. My father was cut off in his prime in his early fifties due to cigarette smoking. He was a strong man and might still have been alive today.

I believe I was within an inch of dying during my 40's although it would have been attributed to a brain haemorrhage rather than to cigarette smoking. I now spend my life being consulted by people who have either been already crippled by the disease or are in the last stages. And, if you care to think about it, you probably know of many too.

There is a wind of change in society; a snowball has started which I hope this book will help turn into an avalanche.

You can help too by spreading the message.

FOR THE BEST IN PAPERBACKS, LOOK FOR THE 🐧

In every corner of the world, on every subject under the sun, Penguins represent quality and variety – the very best in publishing today.

For complete information about books available from Penguin and how to order them, write to us at the appropriate address below. Please note that for copyright reasons the selection of books varies from country to country.

In the United Kingdom: For a complete list of books available from Penguin in the U.K., please write to *Dept EP, Penguin Books Ltd, Harmondsworth, Middlesex, UB7 0DA*

In the United States: For a complete list of books available from Penguin in the U.S., please write to *Dept BA, Viking Penguin, 299 Murray Hill Parkway, East Rutherford, New Jersey 07073*

In Canada: For a complete list of books available from Penguin in Canada, please write to *Penguin Books Canada Limited, 2801 John Street, Markham, Ontario L3R 1B4*

In Australia: For a complete list of books available from Penguin in Australia, please write to the *Marketing Department, Penguin Books Australia Ltd, P.O. Box 257, Ringwood, Victoria 3134*

In New Zealand: For a complete list of books available from Penguin in New Zealand, please write to the *Marketing Department, Penguin Books (N.Z.) Ltd, Private Bag, Takapuna, Auckland 9*

In India: For a complete list of books available from Penguin in India, please write to *Penguin Overseas Ltd, 706 Eros Apartments, 56 Nehru Place, New Delhi 110019*

Audrey Eyton's F-Plus Audrey Eyton

'Your short-cut to the most sensational diet of the century' – *Daily Express*

Caring Well for an Older Person Muir Gray and Heather McKenzie

Wide-ranging and practical, with a list of useful addresses and contacts, this book will prove invaluable for anyone professionally concerned with the elderly or with an elderly relative to care for.

Baby and Child Penelope Leach

A beautifully illustrated and comprehensive handbook on the first five years of life. 'It stands head and shoulders above anything else available at the moment' – Mary Kenny in the *Spectator*

Woman's Experience of Sex Sheila Kitzinger

Fully illustrated with photographs and line drawings, this book explores the riches of women's sexuality at every stage of life. 'A book which any mother could confidently pass on to her daughter – and her partner too' – *Sunday Times*

Food Additives Erik Millstone

Eat, drink and be worried? Erik Millstone's hard-hitting book contains powerful evidence about the massive risks being taken with the health of consumers. It takes the lid off the food we eat and takes the lid off the food industry.

Pregnancy and Diet Rachel Holme

It *is* possible to eat well and healthily when pregnant while avoiding excessive calories; this book, with suggested foods, a sample diet-plan of menus and advice on nutrition, shows how.

FOR THE BEST IN PAPERBACKS, LOOK FOR THE 🐧

PENGUIN HEALTH

Medicines: A Guide for Everybody   Peter Parish

This fifth edition of a comprehensive survey of all the medicines available over the counter or on prescription offers clear guidance for the ordinary reader as well as invaluable information for those involved in health care.

Pregnancy and Childbirth   Sheila Kitzinger

A complete and up-to-date guide to physical and emotional preparation for pregnancy – a must for all prospective parents.

The Penguin Encyclopaedia of Nutrition   John Yudkin

This book cuts through all the myths about food and diets to present the real facts clearly and simply. 'Everyone should buy one' – *Nutrition News and Notes*

The Parents' A to Z   Penelope Leach

For anyone with a child of 6 months, 6 years or 16 years, this guide to all the little problems involved in their health, growth and happiness will prove reassuring and helpful.

Jane Fonda's Workout Book

Help yourself to better looks, superb fitness and a whole new approach to health and beauty with this world-famous and fully illustrated programme of diet and exercise advice.

Alternative Medicine   Andrew Stanway

Dr Stanway provides an objective and practical guide to thirty-two alternative forms of therapy – from Acupuncture and the Alexander Technique to Macrobiotics and Yoga.

A Complete Guide to Therapy   Joel Kovel

The options open to anyone seeking psychiatric help are both numerous and confusing. Dr Kovel cuts through the many myths and misunderstandings surrounding today's therapy and explores the pros and cons of various types of therapies.

Pregnancy   Dr Jonathan Scher and Carol Dix

Containing the most up-to-date information on pregnancy – the effects of stress, sexual intercourse, drugs, diet, late maternity and genetic disorders – this book is an invaluable and reassuring guide for prospective parents.

Yoga   Ernest Wood

'It has been asked whether in yoga there is something for everybody. The answer is "yes"'   Ernest Wood.

Depression   Ross Mitchell

Depression is one of the most common contemporary problems. But what exactly do we mean by the term? In this invaluable book Ross Mitchell looks at depression as a mood, as an experience, as an attitude to life and as an illness.

Vogue Natural Health and Beauty   Bronwen Meredith

Health foods, yoga, spas, recipes, natural remedies and beauty preparations are all included in this superb, fully illustrated guide and companion to the bestselling *Vogue Body and Beauty Book*.

Care of the Dying   Richard Lamerton

It is never true that 'nothing more can be done' for the dying. This book shows us how to face death without pain, with humanity, with dignity and in peace.

The Penguin Encyclopaedia of Nutrition   John Yudkin

This book cuts through all the myths about food and diets to present the real facts clearly and simply. 'Everyone should buy one' – *Nutrition News and Notes*

The Prime of Your Life   Dr Miriam Stoppard

The first comprehensive, fully illustrated guide to healthy living for people aged fifty and beyond, by top medical writer and media personality, Dr Miriam Stoppard.

A Good Start   Louise Graham

Factual and practical, full of tips on providing a healthy and balanced diet for young children, *A Good Start* is essential reading for all parents.

How to Get Off Drugs   Ira Mothner and Alan Weitz

This book is a vital contribution towards combating drug addiction in Britain in the eighties. For drug abusers, their families and their friends.

The Royal Canadian Airforce XBX Plan for Physical Fitness for Men and The Royal Canadian Airforce XBX Plan for Physical Fitness for Women

Get fit and stay fit with minimum fuss and maximum efficiency, using these short, carefully devised exercises.

Pregnancy and Childbirth   Sheila Kitzinger

A complete and up-to-date guide to physical and emotional preparation for pregnancy – a must for prospective parents.

Alternative Medicine   Andrew Stanway

Dr Stanway provides an objective and practical guide to thirty-two alternative forms of therapy – from Acupuncture and the Alexander Technique to Macrobiotics and Yoga.

Naturebirth   Danaë Brook

A pioneering work which includes suggestions on diet and health, exercises and many tips on the 'natural' way to prepare for giving birth in a joyful relaxed way.

FOR THE BEST IN PAPERBACKS, LOOK FOR THE

A CHOICE OF PENGUINS

Castaway   Lucy Irvine

'Writer seeks "wife" for a year on a tropical island.' This is the extraordinary, candid, sometimes shocking account of what happened when Lucy Irvine answered the advertisement, and found herself embroiled in what was not exactly a desert island dream. 'Fascinating' – *Daily Mail*

Out of Africa   Karen Blixen (Isak Dinesen)

After the failure of her coffee-farm in Kenya, where she lived from 1913 to 1931, Karen Blixen went home to Denmark and wrote this unforgettable account of her experiences. 'No reader can put the book down without some share in the author's poignant farewell to her farm' – *Observer*

The Lisle Letters   Edited by Muriel St Clare Byrne

An intimate, immediate and wholly fascinating picture of a family in the reign of Henry VIII. 'Remarkable . . . we can really hear the people of early Tudor England talking' – Keith Thomas in the *Sunday Times*. 'One of the most extraordinary works to be published this century' – J. H. Plumb

In My Wildest Dreams   Leslie Thomas

The autobiography of Leslie Thomas, author of *The Magic Army* and *The Dearest and the Best*. From Barnardo boy to original virgin soldier, from apprentice journalist to famous novelist, it is an amazing story. 'Hugely enjoyable' – *Daily Express*

India: The Siege Within   M. J. Akbar

'A thoughtful and well-researched history of the conflict, 2,500 years old, between centralizing and separatist forces in the sub-continent. And remarkably, for a work of this kind, it's concise, elegantly written and entertaining' – Zareer Masani in the *New Statesman*

The Winning Streak   Walter Goldsmith and David Clutterbuck

Marks and Spencer, Saatchi and Saatchi, United Biscuits, G.E.C. . . . The U.K.'s top companies reveal their formulas for success, in an important and stimulating book that no British manager can afford to ignore.

FOR THE BEST IN PAPERBACKS, LOOK FOR THE 🐧

A CHOICE OF PENGUINS

Adieux: A Farewell to Sartre   Simone de Beauvoir

A devastatingly frank account of the last years of Sartre's life, and his death, by the woman who for more than half a century shared that life. 'A true labour of love, there is about it a touching sadness, a mingling of the personal with the impersonal and timeless which Sartre himself would surely have liked and understood' – *Listener*

Business Wargames   James Barrie

How did BMW overtake Mercedes? Why did Laker crash? How did McDonalds grab the hamburger market? Drawing on the tragic mistakes and brilliant victories of military history, this remarkable book draws countless fascinating parallels with case histories from industry world-wide.

Metamagical Themas   Douglas R. Hofstadter

This astonishing sequel to the best-selling, Pulitzer Prize-winning *Gödel, Escher, Bach* swarms with 'extraordinary ideas, brilliant fables, deep philosophical questions and Carrollian word play' – Martin Gardner

Into the Heart of Borneo   Redmond O'Hanlon

'Perceptive, hilarious and at the same time a serious natural-history journey into one of the last remaining unspoilt paradises' – *New Statesman*. 'Consistently exciting, often funny and erudite without ever being overwhelming' – *Punch*

A Better Class of Person   John Osborne

The playwright's autobiography, 1929–56. 'Splendidly enjoyable' – John Mortimer. 'One of the best, richest and most bitterly truthful autobiographies that I have ever read' – Melvyn Bragg

The Secrets of a Woman's Heart   Hilary Spurling

The later life of Ivy Compton-Burnett, 1920–69. 'A biographical triumph . . . elegant, stylish, witty, tender, immensely acute – dazzles and exhilarates . . . a great achievement' – Kay Dick in the *Literary Review*. 'One of the most important literary biographies of the century' – *New Statesman*